Drayton Beauchamp

The Village That Time Passed By

Margaret Ross

Margaret Ross

Photographer David Lonsdale

David Lonsdale

Published by The Peebles Press

Front cover photograph of the Reverend Ernest William Peto Betts with his wife Catherine outside Drayton Beauchamp Rectory around 1900 by kind permission of his great-nephew James Evers.

Back cover photograph of the lower section of Drayton Beauchamp parish from the air. Photograph taken between 1979 and 1985 by Dave Lee Travis and reproduced with his kind permission.

An artistic impression of the parish of Drayton Beauchamp by kind permission of my grandson Barney Ross-Smith.

ISBN 978-0-9569846-0-9

Printed in Great Britain by Annodata Print Services, Units C1, C2 and C3, Townsend Industrial Estate, 3 Portland Close, HOUGHTON REGIS, Bedfordshire LU5 5AW
E-mail clive@annodata.co.uk **Website** www.annodata.co.uk

This book is dedicated to the residents – past, present and future - of the parish of Drayton Beauchamp

Contents

Preface

This book has evolved from a suggestion made in the late 1990s by Buckinghamshire County Council that each of the villages in the County should work on a "village project" to celebrate the new millennium. Residents of Drayton Beauchamp, a sparsely populated village and civil parish, discussed the idea for several years at successive Parish Meetings, the population being too small to support a Parish Council. We were enthusiastic and felt that such a project would be both interesting and potentially beneficial to the village. Finding volunteers willing to carry out the work was not easy, however, and it was only in 2007 that I agreed to take on the task while David Lonsdale, a skilled and patient photographer, would assume the role of photographer for the project.

By this stage we could no longer remember exactly which Department had suggested the Buckinghamshire Village Project, whether there had been precise instructions as to how it should be carried out, and what form the finished work should take. We decided therefore that we would carry out as thorough a piece of work as we could. I would endeavour to talk to someone from every house, farm and other dwelling in the parish to find out when and why they had moved to Drayton Beauchamp, whether they had interesting stories to relate about the village, how they felt about living here, and what future plans they might have for themselves and their home. I would also study the history of the parish, seeking out old documents and maps to help me understand what the Drayton Beauchamp of the past might have looked like, who its former residents had been, and what kind of lives they had led. In the meantime, David Lonsdale would take photographs of each property and its residents and invite local people to lend old photographs which might further illustrate what our parish was like in the days before most of the current residents came to live here.

Almost exactly four years later we have at last come to the end of what has proved to be a mammoth task and with more than enough material "to fill a book". Undertaking research presents the risk that it will take on a life of its own and if the original problem in this case was to start the work, a greater problem has proved to be that of disciplining myself to declare it finished. There is always another old will or estate paper to study, another vintage tractor or specialist pig breed website to visit, another graveyard to explore, another report on cesspools and infiltration pits to study, another former resident of the village being discovered and proving eager to be interviewed.

I cannot sufficiently express my gratitude for the generosity of the current residents of 46 properties in the parish who have spent so much time helping me and answering what at times may have seemed odd and never-ending questions. Their names appear in the following pages. The 2010-2011 Electoral Register lists sixty households in the parish and two additional households have not been listed. Of this total of 62, the short-term tenants of three properties were omitted from the project and the owners of these properties (who all live close by) were interviewed instead. A previous long-term resident of one of these cottages provided, however, a vivid picture of his growing up in the village and of life in his family's and his neighbours' cottages. The residents of ten properties did not respond to repeated invitations to take part and three others did not wish any personal details about themselves to be included. The Reverend Elizabeth Moxley, village Rector, and the Reverend Andrew Allen, Curate, kindly checked and corrected the chapter about St Mary the Virgin Church and, together with the Churchwardens, granted me invaluable access to the precious Church Registers of Baptisms, Marriages and Burials.

In addition, nineteen former residents were interviewed and provided a wealth of information and rare photographs about the Drayton Beauchamp of the past. Their names too are recorded in this book and they have my heartfelt thanks. Some who lived in more than one house during their years in the village have been given their own separate chapters.

Others who have never lived here but who have some valuable connection with the parish or some particular expertise and who have helped me greatly include David Mead of Wilstone, Sue and Alby Gillingham of Buckland, and Richard Tregoning whose godfather lived in the village from 1947 until 1964. Anne and Rex Watson of the Buckinghamshire Family History Society, Jill and John Nutkins of Cheddington, David Ridgwell of Hastoe Matters and Jim Dean, formerly of Deans Brothers, have all provided valuable and ongoing help. John T Smith of Cheddington History Society has proved himself a most patient and careful mentor and proof-reader and has offered unfailing support and inspiration from the start.

The staff at the Centre for Buckinghamshire Studies and particularly those in the Archive Room have been a never-failing source of expert help and encouragement. The Buckinghamshire County Archaeologists, the English Heritage National Monuments Record Enquiry and Research Service, Julia Wise (Historic Environment Records Officer for Buckinghamshire County Council), Anne Davies (Historic Buildings Officer for Aylesbury Vale District Council) and Anna Borovikov of BEAMS (The Built Environment Advisory and Management Service) have all helped to clarify and confirm the listings of protected village buildings and other structures. Other specialist help was provided by the Buckinghamshire Coroner, Aylesbury Vale District Council's Legal and Estates Services, the Rothschild Archive, The British Waterways Trust, and the Wendover Arm Trust. David Parfitt, an expert in vintage tractors, helpfully identified a Fordson Model F tractor pulling a plough in a village photograph of around 1920. Keith Bailey of the Buckinghamshire Archaeological Society provided expert explanations for idiosyncratic field names. Jill Fowler and Wendy Austin, local historians, solved the mystery of the location of the fatal accident in 1824 when a flat-bottomed skiff overturned and two girls were drowned, (an accident which took place near Halton, not Drayton Beauchamp as had previously been believed). This accident happened as the girls were returning from an outing to Velvet Lawn near Chequers, a favourite picnic spot of the time.

The Drayton Beauchamp Parish Meeting, its chairman my husband Tom Ross, and its clerk, Meryl Nodes, have shown remarkable patience and encouragement during what may at times have seemed a never-ending process.

Finally, my sincere thanks to David Lonsdale for his wonderful photographic record of the village and his encouragement from the beginning, and to David's family and mine who have had to accept our preoccupation over such a long period with this "small project" which turned into a time-consuming, all-absorbing passion. There will inevitably prove to be errors and omissions in the pages which follow. For these I apologise, trusting that they will be outweighed by the wealth of fascinating material which has been discovered about this lovely village and parish and its people – material which, I believe, should be documented and cherished.

Margaret Ross
Drayton Beauchamp
December 2011

Introduction

Drayton Beauchamp (always pronounced "Beecham" locally) is both a village and a civil parish which extends for just under six miles in length and half a mile in width, and which runs along the Buckinghamshire/Hertfordshire border. Starting at the boatyard just beyond the canal bridge at Puttenham Bottom Lock, the narrow strip parish extends up into the hills where the old summer pastures of the parishes of Aston Clinton, Drayton Beauchamp and Buckland meet. A few houses lie in both directions along the Upper Icknield Way at right angles to the main concentration of houses. Traditionally, the 1400 or so acres which make up the parish provided a combination of woodland, pasture and arable land. Drayton Beauchamp is situated in the Chilterns Area of Outstanding Natural Beauty and sections of the parish lie within The Drayton Beauchamp Conservation Area which was created in 1989. For such a tiny parish there are a surprising number of buildings and other monuments listed as being of special architectural or historical interest – a total of nine houses plus a stable block, a canal bridge and canal lock, all Grade II-listed, and the Grade I-listed church.

A settlement – a"vill" - in and around the location of the modern-day parish of Drayton Beauchamp was already in existence long before William the Conqueror commissioned the Domesday Survey in December 1085. Archaeological finds in the parish include Iron Age, Saxon and a small number of Roman artefacts (although, according to a County archaeologist, because the local residents were friendly, the Romans had no need to build a garrison in the area). During excavations for the A41 Aston Clinton bypass in 2001 an early Saxon cemetery dating from around 600 A.D. was discovered at the top of Tring Hill. Eighteen graves were found there, including that of a wealthy, high-status woman.

According to J J Sheahan the word "Drayton" is derived from the words "ton" – a Saxon settlement – and "dray" – meaning a place where wagons were made, repaired or kept. Wikipedia amends the "wagons" to "sledges", arguing that sledges would have been required to pull heavy loads up the steep hills. "Beauchamp" refers to the de Beauchamp – or "Bello Campo" - family who were first associated with the village in the early thirteenth century.

Before 1086 the vill, with a total of nineteen households, seems to have been divided into three separate parts. Wicga and Aelfric (or Aluric), thanes of Edward the Confessor, and a widow were the main holders of land. Given by William to his powerful half-brother Robert the Earl of Mortain along with almost 800 other manors as the rich reward for his support, the estate's new tenant-in-chief was the feudal baron "Mainou (or "Magno") le Breton", with Helgot of Awliscombe, Leofsige (or Lepsi) and William fitzNigel as his under-tenants. The lands were stewarded by the le Breton family for the Crown until the start of the thirteenth century when William de Beauchamp became Lord of the Manor.

Claims and counter-claims about possession of the manor between the de Drayton and de Beauchamp families – and within the de Beauchamp family itself – were frequent until 1363. In that year John de Cobham, third Baron Cobham of Kent who by then held the manor, granted its reversion to Edward III and his successors. The following year, the king gave the Lordship of the Manor of Drayton Beauchamp to his shield-bearer Thomas Cheyne who died four years later and is buried beneath the chancel in the church. The lordship remained with the Cheyne family until 1728 and accounts of subsequent events can be found in the chapters about the Dower House and Drayton Manor.

Several ancient tracks and roads traverse or run close to the parish – the Iron Age earthwork known as Grim's Ditch, the Upper and the Lower Icknield Way (perhaps dating back to the Neolithic Period although there is some controversy about this), and the Roman Akeman Street. The holloway which separates Drayton Beauchamp from Buckland, the strip parish to the south, and which descends from the valley among the hills at the topmost end of the parish all the way down to the main settlement, was "first constructed by the aboriginal Britons and improved by the Romans" according to George Lipscomb, writing in 1847. Two branches of the Grand Union Canal - the Aylesbury Arm and the Wendover Feeder – pass through the parish, supplied with water by the reservoirs whose construction was started in 1802. The Wendover Arm, opened in 1797, was closed in 1904 because of excessive leaking and has not so far been re-opened although the Wendover Arm Trust is working very hard to restore and re-open it. Of more modern construction, the A41 which briefly meets the Upper Icknield Way around the midpoint of the parish, was formerly the old turnpike road from Aylesbury to Tring. Finally, the A41 Aston Clinton bypass, opened in 2003, also cuts through the parish, separating the main settlement from the southernmost woods, summer pastures and dwellings.

Life in the Drayton Beauchamp of the past was harsh for almost everyone. Low wages, poor and cramped accommodation, and the geographical isolation of the parish would have allowed for few luxuries and little relaxation. Illiteracy was inevitably high despite the night classes run at times by the Rector. Overseers and Guardians of the Poor were appointed annually and distributed small amounts of charity. Housing and livelihoods were dependent on the decisions of the Lord of the Manor – a very different picture from that of the 2011 Census which found that 81 percent of dwellings in the parish were owner-occupied. Non-payment of rent might well result in eviction, with goods and chattels sold and the tenant carried off to the Workhouse. Several village people are recorded as having died in the Aylesbury Workhouse or at "100 Bierton Road" as it was euphemistically known after 1904.

By the time of the 2011 Census, only 2.5 percent of the residents of the parish were involved in agriculture. An examination of the eight censuses between 1841 and 1911 yields fascinating comparative data about parish employment in those seventy years. In 1841 there were seven farmers listed. By 1911 the number had dropped to three. In 1841, 41 men described themselves as "agricultural labourers". By 1911 only 22 did so although an additional ten men were listed as working with cows or horses on farms. Male farm servants had disappeared by 1891. The oldest man listed as still in employment was an 88-year-old agricultural labourer in 1901. The youngest boy was a four-year-old straw plaiter living at Buttermilk Cottages near Puttenham in 1891. In the case of the local women, domestic and farm service provided employment for around twelve women in each of the eight censuses. Straw plaiting was not listed in the 1841 Census, and had disappeared again from the list by 1891. In both 1851 and 1891 there were said to be eight straw plaiters in the parish, but in 1861, 1871 and 1881 there were 33, 35 and 36 respectively. This echoes national figures which confirm that the straw hat manufacturing industry declined sharply towards the end of the nineteenth century after many years of providing paid employment for large numbers of women working from home. The youngest girl in employment in the parish was a six-year-old straw plaiter in 1871, sister to the little boy mentioned above. The oldest woman listed as still working was the 83-year-old housekeeper at Drayton Lodge in 1861 who, when she died four years later, was said in the Church Burial Records to have been a faithful and valued servant to the Jenney family for 55 years.

Before the Domesday Survey, the parish of Drayton Beauchamp fell within the Yardley Hundred, a division based on an area of "one hundred hides" which was used for fiscal, judicial and military purposes. Thereafter it became part of the three Cottesloe Hundreds. These divisions seem to have lost their relevance by the end of the nineteenth century. Parish boundaries have changed over the past century and a half. At the Puttenham end of the parish, Helsthrop (or Helstrope) and Buttermilk Cottages were counted as part of Drayton Beauchamp parish until 1886 when they became part of the Wingrave electoral district. The same year Buckland parish acquired Draytonmead Farm (unoccupied after 1905) where an unfortunate young woman drowned her fourteen-month-old son Cyril in the farmyard well in 1917, perhaps as a result of postnatal depression. Whittle Farm similarly became part of the Tring electoral district. At the southern end of the parish Cholesbury, originally a satellite of Drayton Beauchamp, became fully independent from Drayton Beauchamp in 1541 when it was sold by Robert Cheyne to Chief Justice Baldwin. In 1934 just over two hundred acres, formerly in Drayton Beauchamp, were passed over to the new parish of Cholesbury cum St Leonards.

Over the years as boundaries changed, research is made complicated by the disappearance of addresses from census returns and other records. Further complexity arises from the enumerators' seemingly haphazard meanderings around the parish and the lack of street names or numbers. Often no address is given at all, or a cottage is called after its tenant, or a vague numbering system (1 Village Road, 2 Village Road, etc.) is used but not explained. In addition, ages in the 1841 Census are accurate up to fifteen years and then rounded down to the nearest five. This, combined with the inconsistent spelling of surnames in successive censuses and other records, further complicates the task of establishing who lived where.

Another frustrating mystery which I frequently encountered during the initial months of research for this book was the sudden appearance in the 1838 Tithe Map and Apportionment Document of a man called "William Christopher" who seemed to own vast tracts of land and virtually every property in the parish. The mystery was solved with the discovery that William Christopher was actually William Jenney, husband of Caroline Frances Stewart. Documents record that he had adopted the surname "Christopher" by the summer of 1836 and had reverted to "Jenney" in 1843, presumably for financial or legal reasons. Interestingly, although it was in fact Caroline who was the heiress and Lord of the Manor, I have not so far found any document in which William is not entitled Lord of the Manor and owner of the estates which in fact (but not in the law of that time) were Caroline's. Indeed Caroline's name is rarely mentioned at all until reference is made to her death in 1861 and the succession to the lordship of the manor of "her" heirs Stewart William and Arthur Henry Jenney.

Many children died young in the Drayton Beauchamp of the past (four children in one family in the space of six months in 1841) and cholera struck the community in 1865/6 at the same time as a devastating cattle plague. In 1891 diphtheria hit Drayton Beauchamp, killing at least two children during an epidemic which raged throughout Buckinghamshire. Two deaths from smallpox were recorded in 1823, several from scarlet fever between 1868 and 1871 (three from one family in a period of two weeks), and many from "decline" (i.e. tuberculosis). Farming accidents were not infrequent and are graphically recorded in local newspapers and church records. The seventeen-year-old son of an incapacitated labourer drowned in 1871 "while bathing", although whether in the canal or reservoir is not recorded. Several women died within a very few weeks of childbirth, frequently closely followed by the death of the baby.

Punishment for wrongdoing was severe. A document of 8th October, 1771 talks about the need for the repair of the village stocks at the expense of the Lady of the Manor (Martha Gumley). In 1873 a farm worker absented himself from work for one day and was ordered to pay a fine of £1 with 15s costs or to carry out fourteen days' hard labour. In 1882 John Lovegrove the gamekeeper caught a village man setting traps for rabbits in the churchyard. He was fined £2 plus 13s costs – a huge sum for an agricultural labourer to raise, but perhaps preferable to the one month's imprisonment which was the alternative.

As an antidote to the harshness of villagers' daily lives, the Jenney estate papers give details of "cottagers' and farmers' dinners" paid for by the Lord of the Manor. In 1915, twenty-two "cottagers" were entertained at the Rose and Crown in Tring, drinking mainly ale and stout. Eleven farmers enjoyed the rather more expensive port and sherry at their separate dinner. "Harvest Homes" were enjoyed, and children looked forward to a "day at the seaside" which involved a walk to a sandy area on the edge of the reservoir where there was a pier but no wall. There might be fifty people swimming there on a fine day and many families enjoying a picnic beside the water. Villagers loved this free paradise within walking distance of their homes and spent happy days there. Convivial evenings were spent in one another's cottages, and stories of the several local ghosts were recounted and embellished.

The population has risen and fallen over the years – 191 in 1801, a high of 275 in 1831, a fall to 147 in 1911 and a slight rise to 159 in the 2001 Census. The Posse Comitatus of 1798 lists 47 men in Drayton Beauchamp between sixteen and sixty years of age. The Electoral Register of 2010-11 lists 133 people, both men and women, who were eligible to vote. At a time when many families remained in the parish for generations and incomers tended to come from neighbouring villages rather than further away, intermarriage between village families was common and the same surnames crop up in different cottages again and again over the past two centuries and longer. This would have both strengthened the ties of family loyalty, and also increased the possibility that a child would be offered accommodation in another cottage when the conditions became unbearably cramped in his own home.

The appearance and composition of the parish began to undergo huge changes from the mid-20th century. By 1960 all but two farms with their extensive estates had been broken up and sold as private houses, the smallholdings had almost all disappeared, and a handful of new houses had been built. Adjoining cottages were being converted into larger single dwellings and old farm barns converted into private houses. Most villagers no longer worked locally and cars became essential to provide ready access to work, railway stations, schools, shops, and other amenities. The Drayton Beauchamp of today would be unrecognisable to villagers of even seventy years ago.

Even so, and despite the significant changes which have taken place within the village and parish, we Drayton Beauchamp residents remain perversely proud of the fact that we lack pavements and street lights, mains drainage and a gas supply. We have no public building apart from the church – no shop, pub or village hall. Wendover, Aylesbury, Aston Clinton and Tring are all within a very few miles of us, but we remain a charming, peaceful backwater remembered with great affection by all who have lived here and moved elsewhere. As can be seen from the following pages, although there is sadness at the loss of the farming village that Drayton Beauchamp used to be, it remains a place in which people love to live and which they find hard to leave.

We are indeed a village (and parish) that time has passed by – one of the few which remain.

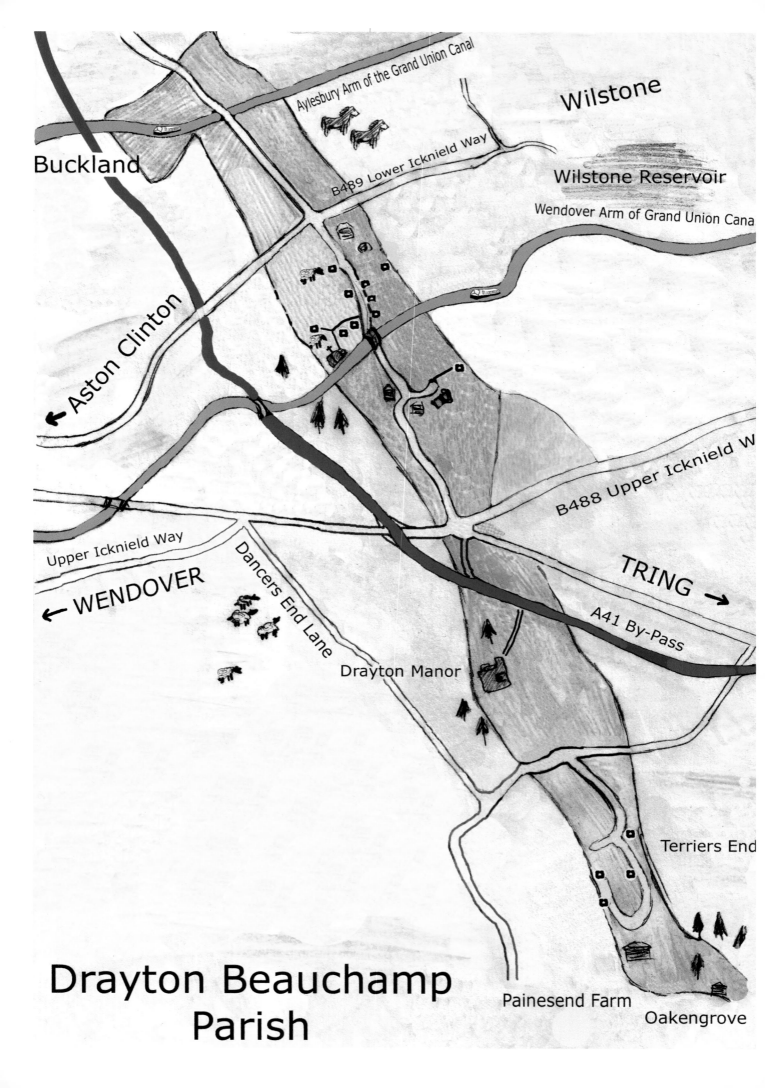

Aylesbury Arm of the Grand Union Canal

Wilstone

Buckland

B489 Lower Icknield Way

Wilstone Reservoir

Wendover Arm of Grand Union Cana

Aston Clinton

B488 Upper Icknield W

Upper Icknield Way

WENDOVER

Dancers End Lane

TRING →

A41 By-Pass

Drayton Manor

Terriers End

Drayton Beauchamp
Parish

Painesend Farm

Oakengrove

Drayton Manor

In May 1728 William Cheyne, Viscount Newhaven, the last of the Cheyne family to live in Drayton Beauchamp, died without a male heir. John Gumley of Isleworth who had made his fortune as a cabinet maker specialising in glassware and particularly mirrors then bought the lordship of the manor of Drayton Beauchamp from representatives of the Cheyne family for £22,200. Manorial rights included the patronage of the village church and the "advowson" – the right to select who would hold the benefice. John Gumley died in December 1728 and his widow Susan /Susanna remained Lady of the Manor until her death in 1750. The couple had three sons and four daughters. John's will directs that the main beneficiaries of his estate apart from his wife should be his younger sons John and Samuel and his daughter Laetitia. Separate, much more modest, provision of a mere £150 a year was made for his eldest son George who had greatly displeased him because of his "profligacy and disobedience".

The old Cheyne manor house with its medieval moats and fishponds near the church was demolished around 1760, and a new manor house, originally called Terret or Turret House, was built within the next decade by the Gumleys to the south of the main village. Village lore has it that bricks from the old manor house were incorporated in the new building, but no evidence has been found to support this.

John Gumley the younger died in India in 1743 and his wife Martha in 1748. A monument to John and Martha still stands in St John's Church, Kolkata (formerly Calcutta). This monument describes Martha as having "concluded this life in a becoming resignation the 21st of August 1748". John's absence abroad and his premature death mean that he is unlikely to have had much, if any, involvement in the Drayton Beauchamp estates. The Gumley family retained Gumley House in Isleworth until it was put up for auction in 1835 and they seem to have spent much of their time there and at their various other properties in London, but Samuel retained the estate and lordship of the manor of Drayton Beauchamp. He died in Belgium in 1763, bequeathing in his will all of his personal estates in Drayton Beauchamp to his wife Martha. In 1769 Martha, named on the "Clergy of the Church of England" database as patron of the village church, was said to be residing in Drayton Beauchamp - presumably in the new manor house. She died in 1788, by which time she was living in Grosvenor Square, London. It is known, however, that the future King George IV as a minor lived for some time at Turret House, receiving tuition from Dr John Lockman, Rector at the time, and in the charge of the man who was his equerry from 1780 until 1786 and from 1787 until 1797. This equerry was Viscount Gerard Lake who was Laetitia Gumley's son and who served as Member of Parliament for Aylesbury from 1790-1802. Indeed, the Universal British Directory of 1791 describes "a new red, brick-built house" – Turret House - which "stands on a hill" and is "inhabited by General Lake, MP for the Borough of Aylesbury." He is known to have lived there for at least another sixteen years. Viscount Lake died in 1808 in London. He and his wife Elizabeth (who predeceased him by twenty years) are buried in a vault beneath the chancel in St Michael and All Angels Church, Aston Clinton.

On Martha Gumley's death in 1788, manorial rights passed to her niece Mary (née Digges), whose late husband – killed in 1782 - was Lord Robert Manners. (A portrait of Mary painted by Allan Ramsay shortly after her marriage in 1756 hangs in the National Gallery of Scotland in Edinburgh.) On Mary's death in 1829 aged 92 her heir was her daughter Lucy (born in 1764) whose two brothers and sister had all died childless. Lucy died in London in 1835, leaving as her heir Caroline Frances Stewart - Lucy's cousin and Mary's great-niece. Caroline was also a granddaughter of Lady Caroline Manners, by that lady's first husband Sir Henry Harpur of Calke Abbey in Derbyshire. Caroline Stewart's husband was Captain William Jenney.

By 1835 the mansion was occupied by Captain William Stanhope Badcock who had been a midshipman at the Battle of Trafalgar. William's wife Selina died in 1838. Selina's brother was the Reverend Henry Harpur Crewe who in 1827 married Frances Caroline, daughter of William Jenney. In the 1838 Tithe Map and accompanying Apportionment Document, William Christopher (61), who had moved from Derbyshire to Drayton Beauchamp in mid-1837, is named as the owner of Drayton Lodge (as Turret House was now sometimes being called). He was owner, too, of all of the farms and cottages in Drayton Beauchamp with the exception of Lock Cottage, and of much of the land in the parish. As outlined in the Introduction, William Christopher was in fact William Jenney, Caroline's husband. William, born in 1779, died in 1859 and Caroline in 1861. Of their six children, Caroline's joint heirs were their two sons Stewart William (1816 - 1904) and Arthur Henry (1819-1894). Interestingly, in 1863 Stewart William married Maria Williamson, one of the seven children of Christopher and Elizabeth Williamson who were tenant farmers at Manor Farm from around 1847 until 1855.

The final Jenney heir was Stewart William's son, also called Stewart William, who was born in 1886 and inherited in 1904. Drayton Lodge remained the home of the Jenney family until early 1909, by which time Stewart William Jenney seems to have been lodging at the Rose and Crown in Tring. In September 1910 his possessions were moved out of Drayton Lodge and the Reverend Walter Neame, a retired clergyman from Padbury, became tenant of the now-unfurnished house along with his niece Constance and five servants. In 1925 Reverend Neame gave permission for a garden fête, organised jointly with Buckland, to be held in the grounds. A second fourteen-year lease was drawn up in 1926 but never came into force owing to the sudden death of Reverend Neame in 1927 from complications associated with appendicitis. Frank Rich took over the tenancy of what seems to have been by then a property in need of considerable modernisation and repair. Indeed, Constance Neame described it in 1927 as a "sink for money". Stewart William Jenney continued to own land and properties in Drayton Beauchamp although these were gradually sold, the estate as a whole being described as having by then no money in hand for repairs. Drayton Manor remained in the ownership of the Jenney Estate until 1976 but Stewart William Jenney himself lived in various places – Tring, Aston Clinton, and latterly Buckland, where he died in 1948. The Jenney estate (which had extended to 586 acres in 1873) seems to have encountered very rough waters financially which began towards the end of the nineteenth century when Stewart William Jenney senior became financially involved with the "Conservative Benefit Building Society" or "Conservative Land Society" – a scheme formed in 1852 by the Tories to buy land and divide it into small plots, each worth at least £50. Houses were built on these plots and sold to professional people who would then be classed as freehold owners, enfranchised, and expected to vote for the Conservative party. This Society, one of many formed at the time to exploit a loophole in the 1832 Reform Act, was wound up by order of the High Court in 1890, presumably resulting in financial loss for those who had contributed. In 1898 the Court of Chancery directed that the Jenneys' Drayton Beauchamp estate should be auctioned. This does not appear to have taken place but there is evidence that money had to be borrowed by the Jenneys on more than one occasion between 1899 and 1910. The financial problems mounted over the next forty years, exacerbated by the younger Stewart William Jenney's ill health and the resulting need for the village Rector, the Reverend Burkitt, and a Tring solicitor, Arthur Vaisey, to administer his affairs.

Arthur William, another of the grandsons of William and Caroline, married Frances Caroline Harpur-Crewe of Norfolk. Of their three children (who changed their surname from Jenney to Harpur-Crewe for inheritance reasons), one son, Henry, inherited Calke Abbey in Derbyshire while their daughter, Airmyne, remained patron of St Mary the Virgin Church in Drayton Beauchamp until her death in 1999.

Drayton Manor, as it is now known, is formed of two wings under a slate roof, the original three-storey square brick-built building with cellars beneath, and a two-storey, semi-circular north wing added a century later. A matching south wing and some offices were demolished, according to J J Sheahan, in 1832 after the death of Mary Manners. The building is Grade II listed.

The stable block (also Grade II listed) to the west of the house dates from the early nineteenth century and is constructed of yellow brick with a slate roof. This building, which would always have incorporated living quarters for the coachmen/grooms, was converted into a self-contained cottage several years ago by the current owners of Drayton Manor and is now rented to private tenants. At some time in the past an imposing barn near the stable block and a glazed conservatory adjoining the house were pulled down.

The walled kitchen garden, formal gardens, and remains of the park all date from the nineteenth century. Thomas Bateman, a gardener at Drayton Manor for many years, lived at the Lodge with his wife Elsie. He knew and loved every inch of the grounds and even after he retired he often returned to sit in the gardens in which he had laboured for so long. The kitchen garden was extensively cultivated during and after the Second World War when Drayton Manor was used as a hospital and rehabilitation centre for injured servicemen ("Drayton Manor Auxiliary Hospital") including the soldier Will Collier from Hang Hill who went there after being injured. Around 1950 and after all the patients had left, the Manor provided temporary accommodation for a group of young visually impaired children whose school in London had been destroyed by bombs.

A second house, built as the Lodge to Drayton Manor, sits at the end of the quarter-mile driveway which leads from Drayton Manor to the B4365 Aylesbury-Tring road. Constructed in 1910, this Lodge was also part of the Jenney estate. Originally built by Stewart William Jenney to house a member of the Reverend Neame's staff, it was sold around thirty years ago to the then owner of Painesend Farm who used it as accommodation for farm workers. It is now privately owned and was redesignated in recent years as lying within Dacorum boundaries rather than in the Aylesbury Vale Electoral District.

In 1958, Drayton Manor was rented by Michael and Maria Relph, he a filmmaker and she an actress. Although they moved away in 1976, both are buried in the village churchyard – as are Michael's parents George and Mercia (Swinburne), both actors. It seems likely that it was during the Relphs' tenancy of Drayton Manor that a fête was held there to which David Mead of Wilstone and Peter Smith of Hang Hill both remember being taken as children. David vividly recalls the thrill of watching real Cossacks displaying their prowess on horseback: feats which he later tried - but failed - to reproduce on his bicycle!

Shirley Read

In the summer of 1976, having spent nine years in New Zealand and whilst living in Aldbury, Colin and Shirley Read bought Drayton Manor and its grounds from the Jenney estate. They were attracted by the space and setting, and the opportunity for their daughter to have her own horse. It did not take long to discover that a major programme of repairs and upgrading was essential. Nonetheless they have always loved the house. Colin died in 2003 but Drayton Manor remains the family residence.

Drayton Holloway

On the 1838 Tithe Map and in the accompanying Apportionment Document, a large arable field of twenty-one acres at the top of the Holloway where it meets the Upper Icknield Way is called Upper Rye Hill. Owned by William Christopher/Jenney, it was being rented in 1838 by John Parrott who was tenant of both Lower Farm and Morgans Farm and a total of 476 acres. In 1919 Leonard Lewin bought this field from William Jenney's grandson Stewart William Jenney the younger, who was by then Lord of the Manor, along with Morgans Farm, seven cottages and 235 acres. Two years later he sold the whole estate to Leslie Webb. In 1926, Upper Rye Hill was sold before the auction of the Morgans Farm estate by Leslie Webb's representatives to James Moor Long who soon afterwards sold it for £583 to Filmer Miles Kidston of Manor Farm, Wingrave.

In 1930 Bessie Florence Horwood of Hastoe Villa, a niece of Major Stewart William Jenney, bought from Mr Kidston for £800 the portion of Upper Rye Hill on which Drayton Holloway, Drayton Holloway Lodge, Beeches Bungalow and two large poultry buildings now stand.

Drayton Holloway and the lodge next door to it, brick-built houses, were constructed for Bessie Horwood on part of this land by William Huckvale junior whose father, also called William Huckvale (1848-1936), had been employed by the Rothschild Estate as an architect and builder. Huckvale houses, of which there are many fine examples in Buckinghamshire and Hertfordshire, are known for their individuality and distinctive features. The gardens were laid out at the same time. During the building process, Bessie, having returned with her younger sister Helen from a trip to India in early 1932, lived at a hotel in London. The lodge had already been completed by 1931 and first appears on the Electoral Register of that year.

For the first twelve years the house was called Holloway House. For several years Bessie Horwood shared it with her mother Elizabeth Jenney (born Elizabeth Batchelor in 1864). Elizabeth, whose name is engraved on the servants' bell board in the house, was the widow of Captain Henry Jenney, Stewart William Jenney's younger brother who died in 1929. Elizabeth's first husband, Charles Horwood, had died aged only thirty-one in 1898, leaving her with two young daughters, Helen and Bessie. In 1950 Bessie Horwood sold the house and land to Thomas Sole, a Surveyor and Land Agent, moving with her mother Elizabeth to Boxhill. Bessie Horwood, who never married, died in Tring in 1953. Elizabeth Jenney lived to the wonderful age of 99, dying in Tring in 1963.

In 1957 Thomas Sole leased out the area of land at the far end of the estate, finally selling this land two years later. In 1967 Lodge Cottage and Drayton Holloway were sold as separate dwellings for the first time.

Dalton (Don) and Margaret Hunt

Don and Margaret Hunt bought Drayton Holloway in 1967 from Thomas Sole who, with his wife Jean, had inherited an estate in Aberdeenshire called Glenbuchat (colloquially known as "Glenbucket"). Drayton Holloway had been on sale as a small estate with lodge cottage and fourteen acres (three acres of which were sold several years later to the then owners of Rye Hill Farm). All but the lodge cottage was bought by the Hunts who moved there from Hayling Island with their son, nine, and two daughters, ten and two. Don is originally from Derbyshire. Margaret, born in Lincoln, discovered after moving to Drayton Beauchamp that several generations of her ancestors had in fact been born, had lived and had died within a very few miles of the village.

The Hunts modified the house slightly from its original layout by connecting the large wooden office to the house. This created an office wing separated physically and psychologically from the main house by a hardwood door, and a guest suite where visiting business associates and friends could be accommodated. From there Don, whose training was as an engineer and who had previously worked in the UK and USA at a high level in mainly engineering firms, ran the business he had established in 1965 offering consultancy to major international firms. This business, combined with the raising of their family, absorbed much of both his and Margaret's time and energy for many years and led to lasting friendships, again often internationally.

Originally attracted to the area and to the house because of its ready access to railway lines, motorway and airports, Margaret's discovery of her local family roots and the couple's many happy years of residency have led them to be certain that Drayton Holloway is where they wish to remain. They enjoy an active, satisfying lifestyle and are in constant contact with their children who all live in the vicinity.

Drayton Holloway lies at the top of the village lane on the Upper Icknield Way facing south and is therefore somewhat separate from the main settlement. The Hunts like the village but note the lack of a social centre. They believe strongly that the church should be used as a village meeting place. This would have the dual beneficial effects of putting the building to regular and varied practical use and of encouraging a greater number of residents to become active members of the village community.

Lodge Cottage

Lodge Cottage sits next to Drayton Holloway facing on to the Upper Icknield Way, and was commissioned in 1931 by Bessie Horwood before the building of Drayton Holloway began. This lodge, presumably also built by William Huckvale junior, was known at first as "New Lodge" and appears on the Electoral Register of late 1931, several months before Elizabeth Jenney took up residence in Holloway House.

For several years Elizabeth Jenney lived in Holloway House/Drayton Holloway along with her daughter Bessie Horwood. During this time, Lodge Cottage was occupied by James Webb and his family but ownership remained with Elizabeth Jenney. In 1950 she sold Drayton Holloway, Lodge Cottage and several acres of land to Thomas Sole, a Surveyor and Land Agent.

In 1967 Lodge Cottage was sold separately from the rest of the estate for the first time. The current owners have lived there since 1996.

DRAYTON HOLLOWAY

Don & Margaret Hunt

BEECHES BUNGALOW

Derrick & Kathy Rollings

RYE HOUSE

Janice & Neil Fuller

Beeches Bungalow

In December 1950 Bessie Horwood, as described in the preceding chapters on Drayton Holloway and Lodge Cottage, sold both of these houses and the piece of land she owned which ran alongside the Upper Icknield Way from the top of the Holloway almost as far as the north-eastern boundary of the parish.

In 1957 Thomas Sole, the new owner of the houses and land, gave permission for around 3 acres of the land beyond Lodge Cottage to be used by Roger Pike and his father so that they could keep chickens whose eggs they then sold to Deans Brothers. (The original Deans business had been started in the 1920s from his cottage in Gubblecote by William Dean, an "eggler" with a horse and cart who collected eggs from smallholders and sold them door to door. His sons then formed "Deans Brothers." in the 1930s.) It is likely that the Pikes constructed the two large poultry buildings which still stand but which are no longer used for poultry-rearing. When Roger Pike moved to a farm some miles away around 1959, Thomas Sole sold the land and poultry buildings to the Pritchard brothers who had a bakery business in London but who both lived within twenty miles of Drayton Beauchamp. They too sold their eggs to Deans, who had no chickens of their own but who were a marketing company, buying eggs from farmers and individuals across a wide area.

Deans amalgamated with Grossmiths, their biggest suppliers, subsequently selling the company to Dalgety in 1969 but keeping the Deans name. Around 1975 Deans bought the farm from the Pritchard brothers and a prefabricated bungalow was erected beside the poultry buildings. This was used to house the manager or as a temporary home for new employees of what became known as Deans Poultry Farm. Day-old chicks would be brought in from hatcheries and reared for eighteen weeks before being distributed to either battery or free-range farms. In 1991 Peter Dean, a grandson of William, bought Deans back from Dalgety and in 2006 amalgamated with Michael Kent of Stonegate to form Noble Foods Ltd..

Derrick and Kathleen Rollings

In recent years, Beeches Bungalow has been rented out privately by Peter Dean, and Derrick and Kathleen Rollings have been tenants since May 2009. Kathy comes originally from Garston near Watford. Derrick comes from Stanford in Lincolnshire but moved as a teenager with his family to Watford where he worked alongside his father in the latter's house-building business. Kathy and Derrick met when both were seventeen, married 48 years ago, and have lived in various places depending on where Derrick's building work has taken them. For several years, Kathy and her sister travelled to Horticultural Shows all over the country demonstrating and selling a flower-arranging device called "Simply Garlands" which her sister had invented.

Kathy and Derrick spent twelve years in Pitstone and indeed have strong links to this area as Derrick's great-grandfather lived in Wilstone and his name is on the War Memorial there – Frank John Payne, Private in the 2nd Battalion of the Bedfordshire Regiment; killed in action on 11th July, 1916.

From Pitstone, the couple lived briefly in Lincolnshire before moving to Arizona. After nine years in the United States of America, Derrick and Kathy returned to England in May 2009. Their adult son and daughter who both spent time in the United States have also settled back in England. Looking for a home to rent, the couple noticed the "To Let" sign outside Beeches Bungalow when driving past and have been living there ever since.

Beeches Bungalow is small – around 900 square feet – with three bedrooms, one public room and a small garden. The property shares a driveway with the poultry buildings and an old air raid shelter which may very well have been built at the request of Bessie Horwood for use during World War II.

The views from the rear of the bungalow - over Wilstone Reservoir, the village, and the countryside beyond - are stunning. Derrick and Kathy hope to stay indefinitely at Beeches Bungalow. They enjoy living (with their cat) in a rural setting and although Kathy does not have a car, good friends visit and the couple's two children are in close contact. They consider the main part of the village to be beautiful but so far have met few people who live there.

Rye House

This single-storey dwelling is believed to date back to 1937 when Bernard and Violet Banfield bought from Fred Green of Bridge Farm a strip of land parallel to the Wendover Arm of the Grand Union Canal and built a house on it. In the Electoral Registers of 1937-9 the Banfields are listed as living at Bridge Farm but this was in fact not the case, the error possibly being made because the Banfields' new house had not yet been given an "official" address. There had been no building on the site before this and the land, part of a large field called "Pye's Hill" owned by the Jenney Estate and tenanted by John Parrott in 1838 when the Tithe Map and Apportionment Document were drawn up, had always been purely agricultural. There was, it seems, no entry from the Upper Icknield Way at that time, and an access driveway was created leading from the Holloway. On higher ground overlooking this driveway now stand Broadview Farm and Broadview House. As there were no Electoral Registers between 1939 and 1945 it is not known exactly when the Banfields left and Clara and Reginald Stevens arrived, but they are certainly registered in October 1946 as living in the house, which by this time was called "Greenpath". This name would have been taken from two tracks, both called Greenpath, and shown on old maps as meeting at right angles close to the house.

The Stevenses moved to Astrope, and in 1950 Annie, Arthur and Eileen Smith appear on the Electoral Register at Greenpath. In 1958 they were replaced by James Gulliford, joined the following year by Eva. James Gulliford apparently owned fruit and vegetable shops in London, in which he sold produce from the fruit trees and bushes, greenhouses and vegetable beds at Greenpath, many of which still exist. The Gullifords seem to have lived largely in London, using Greenpath as a weekend cottage and employing Mick Anns' mother Margery to help with cleaning. By October 1971 Paul and Brenda Scantlebury had taken over the house, remaining there until August 2007 when the present owners, Janice and Neil Fuller, bought the property. Sometime between October 1984 and October 1985 the name of the house was changed to "Rye House".

Rye House sits in fifteen acres of land, ten of which are woodland purchased by Mr Scantlebury only ten years ago. Mr Scantlebury also closed the old driveway which leads straight into the Holloway and retained ownership of it until 2008, when he finally sold it to the Fullers. He had also retained ownership of an acre of land to the side of the driveway on the Upper Icknield Way, selling it somewhat earlier to the owners of Rye Hill Farm. This may be the site of the mink farm which local people remember. The county boundary between Buckinghamshire and Hertfordshire runs through the gardens. This means that Rye House has two postcodes, one for each county.

The external walls of the house are partly of old stone, partly of cavity wall construction. The house has been extended over the years, most recently in the early 1980s with the construction of a large living room. The property now consists of four bedrooms, two public rooms and a study. The present owners have recently secured permission to extend the house upwards.

Neil and Janice Fuller

Neil and Janice Fuller moved to Rye House in August 2007, attracted to a property which they believed had huge potential but which could be lived in comfortably in the meantime. Both originate from Essex and met around 28 years ago in Dagenham. They have moved several times, partly because of Neil's work and partly because they enjoy buying a property which is in need of upgrading and attention, and moving on when the work is completed. Neil works as an accountant based in Milton Keynes and Janice, trained in secretarial work, currently works in a voluntary capacity on the reception desk of the Iain Rennie Hospice at Home. They have two adult children, one of whom still lives at home.

Because of the isolated location of Rye House with no near neighbours and no "passing traffic", the couple perhaps inevitably do not feel themselves to be part of Drayton Beauchamp village although they enjoy coming to Parish Meetings and feel that to hold them in someone's house adds to the relaxed, welcoming atmosphere. They have friends in various places with the majority in Marlow, the town in which they lived when their daughter and son were small. They describe Drayton Beauchamp as a pretty, well-kept village and feel that its character could be spoiled if rather unnecessary "amenities" such as a pub or shop were added.

"Tring Hill"

Nine houses, close to the top of the Holloway but separated from the lower part of Drayton Beauchamp by the Upper Icknield Way and now also by the A41 Aston Clinton bypass, sit in a row within the parish boundaries. The house nearest the Holloway is situated above and very near the bypass. All nine are in the area in which human remains and artefacts dating from early Saxon times were discovered during the excavations for this new dual carriageway. The houses face on to Tring Hill and have panoramic views at the rear over the Vale of Aylesbury.

The house nearest the Holloway is called The Crest. Alongside are Broadlands, Domus, Shepherds Gate, Buckland View, Norvic, Red Roof, Highclere and Tinkers Hey. Some are bungalows, some two-storey dwellings, all with tiled roofs. The oldest appears to be The Crest, which first appears on Electoral Registers in 1931. Broadlands is listed from 1935 and Domus (originally called "Dormers") from 1936. There would appear to have been some re-naming of houses over the years as several names disappear and others take their place. One couple lived at Broadlands for fifty years. Another couple lived together at Domus for the same length of time, with the widow of the couple remaining in the house for a further eight years after her husband died.

No resident from any of these houses responded to invitations to take part in this project. This may be of no significance, but it would suggest that the geographical isolation of these houses has given rise to the lack of a feeling of emotional connection to the parish of Drayton Beauchamp.

Terriers End

Terriers End, originally two cottages, may date back as far as 1680 but no documentary confirmation of this has so far been discovered. Built of old bricks and heavily timbered, the slope of the roof and the dormer windows make it likely that the house was originally thatched although it is now tiled. The cottages were often used to house workers employed at Painesend Farm.

The origin of the name "Terriers End" is uncertain. The Reverend William Hastings Kelk in his 1854 history of Drayton Beauchamp writes with conviction that the house, like Painesend, was called after a previous owner or resident. An expert from the Buckinghamshire Archaeological Society is of the same opinion. The Quaker Minutes Book of 1673 announces "the intention of marriage of Thomas Morton of Tarriers End in the parish of Draiton Beacham and Mary Coley of Tring". (Ten years later Thomas Morton is again mentioned in this book, but this time because he has been "presented and indicted for being absent from Church for three months".) In Bryant's 1824 map of Buckinghamshire the house is called "Tyger's End". In the 1838 Tithe Map and Apportionment document, an arable field near the house is called "Tyer's" and an orchard beside the house is called "Tyer's End". In the 1841 Census, it is called "Tayers End" but by the 1861 Census this has become "Terriers End".

A horse-drawn single track railway used to run up the valley past Terriers End. The track continued below Painesend Farm through the field to the deep valley or coombe known as The Crong and to the Dancersend Pumping Station owned by Lord Rothschild. This railway carried lime to soften the water and coke to run the twin beam engine built in 1867 by James Kay of Bury. A rail was turned up some years ago by a combine harvester working near Terriers End.

Beside the house runs a holloway – a continuation of the holloway which runs through the lower part of the parish. It passes close to Drayton Manor but pre-dates it by several centuries. Traditionally, holloways would have been used by cattle and pig herdsmen and by sheep drovers as they moved their livestock up to the high pastures for the summer and back down again for safekeeping in the lower pastures during the winter. The regular passage of men and animals would have kept these ancient holloways free from invasive weeds and scrub.

On the other side of this lane and featured in old photographs was a thatched cottage. Old records frequently do not differentiate between the two Terriers End cottages, the thatched cottage, and Fiddlers Green which is the nearest house further along the lane. For instance, in 1767 "a cottage at Terriers End" was purchased by William Butcher of Little Tring, yeoman, from Thomas Woodman. Which cottage this means is not specified, but it appears to have been sold again in 1801 to Lady Robert Manners (Mary). In addition, William and Alice Capel and subsequently Emanuel and Mary Gillingham are listed in Church and Electoral Registers as living at Terriers End, but it would appear that from around 1913 until 1923 the Capels and after them the Gillinghams lived in the thatched house rather than at Terriers End. Even as recently as 1950, the Ordnance Survey map does not distinguish between the various properties.

In the 1838 Tithe Map this thatched house is described as a "cottage, garden, barn and yard." The owner was William Jenney and the tenant was John Choules of Painesend Farm whose gruesome death is described in the chapter about Painesend Farm. Emanuel Gillingham, born in 1876, who lived there from 1924 until 1929 with his wife Mary Ann and several children, collected animal intestines from butchers and slaughterhouses and took them back to the barn behind the cottage where they were cleaned and preserved before being returned to butchers to be used as sausage casings. By March 1928 the Gillinghams had moved to a bungalow in Buckland with a bigger building alongside it in which Emanuel established a family business of the same kind – described in some detail in the Book of Buckland. This workplace (timber framed and with asbestos sheeting sides and a concrete floor) was very cold, and Buckland residents remember seeing members of Emanuel's large family walking to and from work wearing headscarves, woollen mufflers and thick gloves. The Gillinghams' old home beside Terriers End fell into disrepair and was used by George Jaycock as a shelter for his pigs and chickens. Eventually it collapsed or was demolished in the early 1930s, but the land on which it stood was rented from at least 1881 until 1935 by John Gower, a coal merchant living in Tring.

Although it is impossible to be absolutely sure, it seems highly likely that for several years in the late 18th and early 19th centuries, two particular families lived at Terriers End or in one of the houses included under that heading. Two generations of the Paradine family appear in church records from 1815 until 1871, by which time they were living at Buckland and Little Tring. The Cyster or Syster family were also living at or around Terriers End by 1798, if not earlier, and family members continued to live there for eighty years.

In 1838 the two Terriers End cottages were owned by William Jenney and occupied by William Bull and William Newman. William Bull's name appears on the Cottesloe Hundreds Militia Ballot List of 1812 where he was described as being exempt from service. He was widowed in 1837 and in the 1851 Census was said to be lodging with his daughter Ruth and son-in-law James Baldwin. He died in 1853 aged 83. In the 1841 Census William Newman is listed as 23, a coach builder, with wife Ruth the same age and two very young children. Also living with them were fifteen-year-old Mary Newman (perhaps his sister) and fifteen-year-old Mary Paradine whose parents and several other family members had all died in the space of three years. Another branch of the Paradine family, impoverished and with five children, was at the time living at the Dower House. The Newman family, by then with four children, were still at Terriers End in the 1851 Census but do not appear again in subsequent years although William's name does appear in the London Gazette of 1854. By 1891 Thomas Kirby and his wife Lucy were living at Terriers End, as was the family of Charles Baldwin – James Baldwin's son.

By 1901 Thomas Kirby had died and in the 1911 Census the two tenants were the families of Job Allen, a cowman, and George Smith, a carter, who had taken over Charles Baldwin's tenancy in 1910. Job Allen's father William (who had produced at least nine children) is recorded in the village church's Burial Register as having been "killed instantaneously" in 1873 when, aged 56, he fell from a load of hay. George Smith and his wife Ellen were the parents of Frank Smith and grandparents of Peter Smith of Hang Hill Cottages. After George died in 1915 his widow remarried in 1931 and remained at Terriers End until 1959.

In October 1919 Lucy Kirby bought the two Terriers End cottages from Stewart William Jenney and in 1932 sold them for £350 to Henry and Lucy Jaycock, who had been living at Hang Hill Cottages. Lucy "Tilly" Jaycock was the local washerwoman who did the laundry for the Manor. It is quite likely that she would have drawn the water needed for her work from the well in the front garden of Terriers End – a well which still functions. The bourne which gave rise to the name Duckmore Lane on which Terriers End is situated can still be heard running at the bottom of the well on its way to Tring.

One of the two cottages was sold to Esma ("Molly") Dixon, who first appears at that address on the 1960 Electoral Register. Henry Jaycock died in 1963. After Lucy Jaycock's death, intestate, in 1967, ownership was transferred to her nephew and niece – Edward Jaycock and Gladys Hunt. Neither of the two ever lived at Terriers End and in 1969 they sold their cottage to Esma Dixon. Her son Kay, widowed, had been living nearby with his two sons, but now moved to Terriers End which was enlarged at the west end – a dining room, bedroom and garage being added. Several years later he married his second wife, Marie. Esma Dixon died in 1981 and Kay bought both cottages in 1982, combining them to form one house.

Guy and Elizabeth Moores

Guy and Elizabeth Moores bought Terriers End from Kay and Marie Dixon in March 1999. Guy, born in Bristol, spent most of his career in government publicity and marketing having started out as a commercial artist. Elizabeth was born in Banbury and after university in Liverpool worked as a medical researcher. She later taught biology at Berkhamsted School for Girls for 22 years. The two met through mutual friends, married and then lived in London, Bricket Wood and latterly Berkhamsted for 29 years. They have three daughters and four grandchildren. When Guy retired in 1997 they decided to move into the countryside, finally discovering Terriers End which, although apparently isolated, is actually only one mile from Western Road (the old A41) in Tring.

The house now has four bedrooms and the Moores replaced the old "Banbury" garage with a brick-built one. They added a garden room at the west end of the property and enlarged the kitchen by removing a wall and passage from the living to the dining room. They have no further plans for structural changes, and no intention of leaving Terriers End so long as they are able to manage the house and garden - a garden which with their skill and hard work is now one of the most beautiful in the parish.

Guy and Elizabeth describe Drayton Beauchamp as a friendly parish where newcomers are welcomed and neighbourliness is a strong feature. They are involved in village and church affairs, considering an ancient church like St Mary's to be an essential and irreplaceable centre of the community. Terriers End lies between two communities which stretch along the valley, and Guy and Elizabeth feel happily integrated with both. Although there is very little passing vehicle traffic, neighbours around Terriers End tend to walk or ride and are therefore more likely to meet one another than those who live in the lower part of the parish where driving and commuting are more the norm. Guy and Elizabeth have also maintained strong links with their family and with old friends from school and work.

Painesend Farm

It has not so far been possible to establish a definite year from which the very first Painesend Farm dates, but a building with this name is known to have been in existence for over 400 years, while the name "Payne" appears in parish records even earlier. In 1546, a Thomas Payne was married in the village and a William Payne in 1551. The Reverend Hastings Kelk (Records of Buckinghamshire Part 1, volume 1, 1854) links Painesend Farm to a "William Payne of Paynesend" who is named in the Parish Register of 1584 as having been buried on "ye 5th of October", and the Victoria County History volume 3 asserts that in the 16th century the "farm or lordship of Painsend is referred to as being in the tenure of John Payne". The farmhouse seems to have been rebuilt more than once, and not always in exactly the same position. The spelling of the name, too, varies over time and between documents.

In May 1710 a William Weston the Elder of Paynes End, yeoman, is mentioned in connection with the sale of a close of arable land in Drayton Beauchamp which formed part of the close called Seyers Croft. Interestingly, a field behind the cottages between the Dower House and Upper Farm in the lower part of the parish is named on old maps (the 1838 Tithe Map, for instance) as "Payn's Close". Owned by William Jenney, this field was being rented in 1838 by Thomas Griffin of Upper Farm whereas John Choules was at that time the tenant farmer of Painesend. More exploration would be needed to establish whether this is the close of arable land referred to above in the sale of 1710.

The fields and woods surrounding the farm have strong military connections, particularly to the Civil War. Several field names allude to this – Short Butts, Long Shot, etc. – and also to the fact that archery practice by villagers was actively encouraged. Many artefacts dating back to this time (as well as to Roman times) have been dug up in the area. It is believed that soldiers may have gathered here before marching on Aylesbury or on Berkhamsted Castle. In more recent times, an unexploded German bomb was detonated at Painesend in November 1940, and the following year a German incendiary bomb fell on Hilda's Field, Painesend, but caused no damage.

Other field names illustrate the nature of their use – "Saintfoin" (a species of clover), for instance, or "New Took In". "Smith's Shop Field" may refer to the activities of bygone blacksmiths who would have been kept fully occupied with the making and repairing of farm, horse, and perhaps also military, equipment. The name Hang Hill by which a particularly steep field near Painesend Farm on the Chiltern scarp is known most probably arises - according to an expert in Buckinghamshire field names - from the Old English words "hangel (a slope) or "hangra" (a wood on a steep hillside).

It is difficult to feel confident about who lived where in the Drayton Beauchamp of the past. Censuses and Electoral Registers frequently omit addresses altogether, use one address to cover several separate residences, or number houses in an unexplained way which obscures rather than confirms their location. Painesend is no different in this respect. The address often appears to include several cottages as well as the farmhouse, and some of these – for instance, Little Manse - no longer exist under those names. In addition, many residents shared a surname and no doubt moved from one cottage to another over time. Young relatives would be taken in as lodgers too, and if a child died, a subsequent baby might well be given the same name.

What is known is that Painesend Farm was owned by Lucy Manners, Lord of the Manor, in 1830, and by her successors the Jenneys when the Tithe Map was produced in 1838, and that it remained as part of the Jenney estate until as recently as 1999. The "farmhouse" was made up of two cottages, occupied in 1838 (and indeed even before then in 1830 when Lucy Manners was Lord of the Manor) by John Choules and his family who originated from Berkshire. Nearby were two tiny cottages (eventually made into one) which shared a well and outbuilding. In 1838 these cottages were tenanted by Joseph Bunce (who died in 1840 aged 74 followed a year later by his widow) and John Choules' son Thomas. Tragically, John Choules (aged 66) was murdered on 21st October 1839 by his best friend Thomas Pattison, in a well-documented case. Thomas, 45, a native of Northumberland, was the father of eight children aged between one and fifteen years, a fellow Guardian of the Poor and a fellow farmer, living as he did at Dancersend within half-a-mile of John. The two men had been drinking heavily for many hours at the New Inn, Bucklandwharf, and set off unsteadily on the one-and-a-half mile walk home around 10 p.m., arm in arm. John seems to have taken a slightly different footpath from Thomas at one stage - perhaps in order to surprise and tease his friend who was known to be afraid of the dark woods alongside this isolated lane. When John then reappeared at a spot called Putnam's Gap where the footpath and Dancersend Lane met, Thomas did not recognise him and in his befuddled state believed he was an assassin sent by Humphrey Bull the Receiving Officer (also, ironically, a good friend of the two men) to kill him. He beat John about the head so severely that the older man died immediately. Thomas, however, still did not realise who his victim was until after he had tried unsuccessfully to persuade Eliza White, cook at Drayton Manor, to waken her master, William Christopher/Jenney and had finally managed to summon help in Tring from the local policeman. When John's identity was confirmed Thomas's remorse and grief were apparently painful to witness. Although found guilty of manslaughter, a recommendation for mercy was made by the jury and he was imprisoned for only seven months.

John's son Thomas Choules married an Elizabeth King in Berkshire in December 1840 but she died a year later shortly after the death of their five-month-old son, John. Thomas remarried in Drayton Beauchamp in 1853 but his wife Elizabeth (née Grover) died three years later aged only 29 and on the same day as their twelve-day-old son Herbert. Thomas was left with a son, two years old, and also called John. In 1858, aged almost fifty, he married Jane Smith, daughter of Job and Mary and 28 years his junior. Thomas himself died only four years later. It is uncertain what happened to Jane and his three surviving children. Jane's much younger brother Amos, however, is recorded as having married Ann Nutkins in 1874 – thereby creating yet another of the many inter-familial links found in the parish. (The name Nutkins first appears in parish church records in 1614.)

The Apportionment Document of 1838 talks about the "site of a cottage" near Painesend owned by William Jenney. From the Tithe Map this appears to have stood at the entrance to Pavis Wood close to Painesend and beside what are identified as a "Potatoe Field" and a "Piece under the Wood". Five further cottages appear to have been considered part of Painesend Farm for use as farmworkers' cottages – the two Terriers End Cottages, the thatched cottage nearby across the Holloway and the two Fiddlers Green cottages.

The present farmyard at Painesend did not appear until the 1960s. An old dairy and milking parlour still stand, and have both been converted into living accommodation. Into a beam in the milking shed has been carved "TC August 11.1855." This must refer to Thomas Choules who by 1841 was farmer at Painesend following the murder of his father two years earlier. Thomas's younger brother William, his farm foreman, died in 1852. Thomas himself died in 1862 and Henry Chapman became tenant farmer at Painesend. (Henry's unfortunate wife Jane died in 1886 when her eleventh child was only five years old.) By 1891 Edwin Grange had replaced Henry Chapman, followed by James Burnham (who did not live in the farmhouse), and in 1896 by the latter's brother-in-law Lot White who _did_ live in the farmhouse, newly renovated for his arrival. (When Lot White left Drayton Beauchamp in 1908 he moved to Moat Farm in Buckland. He died in 1917 and is buried in Buckland churchyard.)

In 1896 there were 118 acres attached to the farm. In 1911 Archibald Chambers became foreman of Painesend, employed by a (Harry) Logan Turner, tenant from 1908, who lived in Tring and who was a veterinary surgeon for the "London North Western Railway" at a time when cattle and sheep were routinely transported by rail. Lime burning was planned as early as 1900, and a pit was apparently dug in the field known as Eldins so as to extract chalk which would then be burnt and slaked with water to form lime. Receipts for 1914 show that Logan Turner was indeed selling lime for which royalties were paid. By 1922, the year which marked the end of Logan Turner's lease, the land attached to Painesend extended to 500 acres. He moved away, dying in 1966 aged eighty, and is buried in Aston Clinton churchyard along with his wife and young son. He was replaced as tenant at Painesend by Edward Littlechild who in turn assigned the tenancy to Bertram Tucker in 1930.

An interesting aspect of Drayton Beauchamp life was the appointment every year until 1939 of two local men to act as village constables. The practice seems to have been that one constable would be resident in the lower part of the parish and the other the current tenant farmer at Painesend. Sadly, the constables' handcuffs and truncheons, popularly believed still to be located somewhere in the parish, are now nowhere to be found.

Dancersend, although in Buckland parish and part of the Parrott estate, seems to have been closely linked over the years with Painesend. A working farm until around 2000, Dancersend was owned for many years by Claud Leach (who died in 1972) and his wife Marnie (who died in 1985). Painesend ran both cattle and sheep until the late 1960s and the shepherd traditionally lived at the westerly side of Dancersend. Henry (Knox) Chapman who farmed at Painesend for many years was not related to the Henry Chapman of the 1860s but *was* related to the Leaches of Dancersend. Brought up at Dancersend, both he and Claud Leach before him farmed Dancersend and Painesend as one holding from the 1930s. In 1999 Gavin Chapman, Knox's son, bought Painesend Farm from the Jenney estate. He in turn sold it in 2005 to Peter and Karin Vallis, the current owners.

Peter and Karin Vallis

Peter Vallis has known Gavin Chapman for many years and has long participated in the shooting and other rural pursuits available on the estate which now extends to 400 acres and includes permanent pasture for grazing neighbouring farmers' sheep as well as arable land and woodland. The soil at the highest reaches is of clay and chalk.

Peter, now retired, had a business supplying commercial fuel for the haulage industry, and lived until recently with his wife Karin in Kings Langley. They have three daughters who all live around Painesend Farm and are fully involved with its life and work. Karin's brother too works there and lives in the nearby cottage. The old farmhouse itself has recently been demolished and a new four-bedroomed home has been built on the site, connecting with the barn beside it which was converted in 2005 and named "Eldins" after an old field nearby. Peter and Karin moved into their new home in September 2011.

Peter sees himself as a "park keeper" for the estate rather than a farmer. Commercial shooting parties are already accommodated and it is planned to have a kitchen garden so that guests can enjoy Painesend's own fruit and vegetable produce. A new borehole has been dug and is yielding exceptionally pure water. A bee-keeping venture is also underway.

TERRIERS END

Guy & Elizabeth Moores

YEW TREE COTTAGE

Mary & Simon Brown

FIDDLERS GREEN

Hilary & Phil Hurst & Family

Yew Tree Cottage

Brick-built in 1610 and with a thatched roof, Yew Tree Cottage was originally a tiny cottage with a barn at one end which served as the workshop for the carpenters who lived in the cottage from at least 1841 until 1920 and who are believed to have carried out all of the carpentry work for the Jenney estate from cradle to coffin. In a document drawn up by the Court of Chancery in 1898 it is described as "a cottage, carpenter's shop, good garden and orchard occupied by Widow Osborn". Estate papers show that the thatch was renewed in 1916 and repaired in 1917 – no doubt a regular expense for the Jenney family with several thatched properties to maintain around their estate. The barn is now the sitting room and the cottage has been considerably extended by its present owners and by their immediate predecessors.

In the Tithe Map and Apportionment Document of 1838, Yew Tree Cottage is listed as being owned by Catharine Lucas and tenanted by James Osborn, a farm labourer and carpenter. In the 1841, 1851 and 1861 Censuses, James and Elizabeth Osborn and their growing family are listed as still living at this address. In 1850 a seventh child, Sarah Ann, was born – followed by two further daughters. Sarah lived her entire life in Yew Tree Cottage, marrying Jabez Harrowell of Tring in 1870. Another Harrowell family who originated from Tring lived in the lower part of the parish from around 1834 but more research would be required to discover whether they were related to Jabez or not.

Jabez moved into Yew Tree Cottage on his marriage to Sarah, remaining there until he died in 1920. Sarah continued to live there until her own death some twelve years later. Elizabeth, Sarah's mother, is the "Widow Osborn" of the 1898 document, and 87 years old in the 1901 Census. She died in 1904 aged ninety, surviving her husband by over forty years.

Jabez and Sarah had no children of their own, but their nephew Frank (who was born in 1900 and who died in 1985) has written that the couple rented their cottage from the Jenneys for £6 per year which was paid on "Drayton Rent Day" – probably Lady Day (25th March). Jabez was a carpenter and joiner whose job it was to look after all of the farms and buildings owned by the Butchers of Butcher's Bank in Tring. These properties were spread over a wide area from Great Missenden to Aylesbury, and Sarah used to wave a lantern at the foot of Crong Wood to guide her husband home with his pony and cart at the end of a long working day.

At some point between 1932 and 1936 Yew Tree Cottage must have been sold by the Jenneys. By 1936 it is listed in the Rate Account Book as being owned by Northchurch Estates Ltd., a property company which was wound up voluntarily in 1962. By 1958 Keith and Jane McDougall, who belonged to the McDougall family of both Rank Hovis McDougall and of Cooper McDougall (now the Wellcome Foundation in Berkhamsted) had taken up residence at Yew Tree Cottage, staying there until 1967 when they moved to Norfolk.

Yew Tree Cottage lies in an area steeped in history. The nearby Icknield Way was an important Roman through route while bones from an Iron Age settlement and more bones believed to be from a battle during the Cromwellian period have been dug up in the grounds of nearby Dancersend.

Simon and Mary Brown

Simon and Mary Brown bought Yew Tree Cottage three days after becoming engaged in February 1967 and moved there in August of that year. Mary comes from Wiltshire and Simon from Surrey, although Simon was brought up during the war in Little Gaddesden where his grandmother lived. Their three children, Veronica, Louise and Philip were all raised in Yew Tree Cottage. The cottage appealed to the family because of its isolated, peaceful and beautiful setting. It was also convenient for commuting to London, where Simon worked as a dealer in antique furniture and as a manufacturer of traditional furniture.

Simon and Mary have always considered themselves fortunate to live in Yew Tree Cottage and love the valley where it lies. This valley is found at the narrowing points of three triangular parishes - Drayton Beauchamp, Buckland and Aston Clinton - and peaks at St Leonards, Buckland Common and Hastoe. The valley has become a community in its own right, being cut off from the centres of the parishes by the A41 and now also by the A41 Aston Clinton bypass. In recent years with Mary's active part in the life of the village church, they have become much more involved with the parish and its residents as a whole. They see Drayton Beauchamp as having changed little over the past forty years and have no plans to leave the house and area of which they are so fond.

Hang Hill Cottages

The four original Hang Hill Cottages probably date from the early 19th century although their exact age is not known. In the 1838 Tithe Map and Apportionment Document, Hang Hill Cottages and a garden of 38 perches are said to be owned by Edward Field and tenanted by George Harrowell and James Wells. James Wells is identified in 1798 on the Posse Comitatus List for Buckinghamshire as a servant aged eighteen and living in Drayton Beauchamp. He died of "dropsy" in 1863, followed by his wife from the same cause only one month later. George Harrowell died in 1878 aged 75.

The official vagueness and contradictoriness shown by the official record-keepers gives rise to particular complications in this part of the parish because of the large number of related individuals who lived in close proximity to each other, and in the case of the Smith family, by the fact that a Smith married a Smith. Two families with the surname Smith were in fact living in this part of the parish as far back as 1851 and the name continues to appear on records for the next 150 years. As if this were not sufficiently complicated, three Nash brothers married three Smith sisters between 1890 and 1902.

Hang Hill Cottages are often listed under the Terriers End or Painesend heading in official documents, although occasionally mentioned by name – for instance in the record of the burial of a young man in 1818. The address is specifically mentioned again in 1823 when a Richard Barefoot died of "decline" and once again in 1834 when his eleven-year-old son (born posthumously) died. Richard Barefoot is also listed on the Posse Comitatus list of 1798 as a labourer aged twenty.

From the 1841 Census onwards, familiar names appear – almost certainly those of tenants living at Hang Hill Cottages – and some of these surnames are present in the parish for many years even before 1841. Among them are Nash (also on the Posse Comitatus list), Dunton, Brackley, Horn, Jaycock and West. The 1891 Census lists the residents of Hang Hill Cottages as the families of Henry Dunton, William Jaycock, Joseph Brackley and James Nash. By 1911 Ellen (Helen) Smith is living there, widowed and with three children. The widowed Mary Nash lives next door with two children, two grandchildren and with Joseph Brackley, also widowed, as a boarder. William Jaycock, his wife and four children live next to Mary Nash, and the widowed Henry Dunton and his two children and grandchildren in the fourth cottage.

In 1911 the Hang Hill Cottages were still owned by the Jenney estate, but by January 1912 the Valuation List for the parish of Drayton Beauchamp lists Lord Rothschild as owner. It is likely that the cottages were sold again as part of, or shortly before, the 1938 Tring Park Estate auction. Indeed in the 1936 Rate Account Book, the four cottages are said to belong to Mrs M M A Hearn and Peter

Smith remembers during his childhood a Mr Hearn who lived in the Wigginton area and who used to collect the rent once a month by donkey cart. The two Hang Hill Cottages are now owned by Simon and Mary Brown of Yew Tree Cottage and rented out.

Peter Smith

Peter Smith was born in 1936 to Francis (Frank) and Rose Smith. Frank's parents, Ellen and George, are listed on the 1911 Census as living at Terriers End. George died at a young age, and Ellen eventually remarried, her second husband being Fred Cutler, himself a Drayton Beauchamp man. Peter's maternal grandparents, also with the surname Smith, lived at Hang Hill Cottages.

Rose and Frank Smith lived in Tring after marrying, but when Frank went overseas as a Gunner with the Royal Artillery during the Second World War, Rose moved back with the three-year-old Peter to Hang Hill Cottages to be with her mother Helen who had also been widowed while still a young woman. Frank survived Dunkirk but died aged 34 on 28th March 1945 just before the war ended and while he was still in the Army. He is buried in Tring Cemetery and honoured on the Tring War Memorial.

By 1937, Claud Leach had bought Dancersend. He also rented Painesend Farm from the Jenney estate and in the early 1950s bought the four "two-up, two-down" Hang Hill Cottages – presumably from Mr Hearn. Soon after buying them, Claud Leach modernised them and converted the four into two. Peter's family had always lived in the cottage farthest from the farmhouse but shortly before modernisation began they moved into the cottage nearest the farmhouse to look after Will Nash, now widowed, and like a grandfather to Peter. (Will was one of at least seven children born to James and Mary Nash, and appears on the 1891 Census as a six-year-old. His three older brothers married the three Smith sisters.) Will looked after the pigs at Dancersend and kept his own in the field behind the cottages.

Peter's cousin Derrick Smith and his wife Gladys, meanwhile, moved into Peter's former home. After the modernisation of the cottages Peter, his mother and Will Nash all moved back into Peter's old home, now extended and called "2 Hang Hill Cottages". Knox Chapman and his wife lived for a while at 1 Hang Hill Cottages but after Knox left the Army and took on the farming tenancy of Painesend, Archie West (who had been a cook sergeant in Knox's regiment) and his wife Christine moved into number 2. Archie was the gardener at Dancersend, but his home vegetable patch at Hang Hill was particularly productive too, lying as it did on a thick bed of silt from an old stream. Archie, widowed in 1985, continued to live there until his death in 2002 at the age of 94.

As a boy, Peter cycled to school in Tring (as did all of the children at the top end of the parish) and his friends lived either in Tring or in the top reaches of Drayton Beauchamp around Hang Hill. He rarely came to the lower end of the parish, but remembers that each year on Whit Monday he, along with his family and neighbours, would walk to the village church where envelopes of money were distributed under the terms of a village charity. This was still continuing at the end of the war. He remembers too the "Victory Party" in the Schoolhouse in 1947/8, and the fair at Drayton Manor where the Cossacks on horseback appeared (the same event which inspired the young David Mead of Wilstone to attempt to re-enact the Cossacks' feats later on his bicycle).

Peter started work at Painesend and Dancersend as soon as he left school aged fifteen and continued there for fifty years. The two farms originally extended to around 300 acres with seven farm workers, two of these being cowmen employed simply to look after 24 cows. Peter remembers the Painesend Farm of his childhood as a brick-built single dwelling, extended slightly when Knox Chapman came to live there in the early 1960s.

Peter recalls the workforce in the early 1950s as comprising Will Nash of Hang Hill Cottages, Fred Gray from Tring, Stan Collier (one of the cowmen), Stan Hunt (the second cowman) and the latter's son Reg all living at Painesend Farm Cottages, Alfred Bryant the farm manager or bailiff, and Peter himself. By the time Peter retired in 2001, the estate had grown to 500 acres because of the acquisition of land which had formerly been part of the Drayton Manor estate, but the mechanisation of farming and the gradual reduction in the number of farm workers meant that Peter eventually found himself as the only person employed - even milking 120 cows by himself. He had worked under three farmers – Claud Leach, Knox Chapman and Gavin Chapman, and had seen the separation of Painesend from Dancersend. By the time Peter was about forty, the animals had all gone too – cows, sheep and pigs – and the arable farming (notably of barley) was all being carried out by contractors.

Peter met his wife Sylvia after she came south from Northumberland to work as a nanny at Uplands, near Dancersend. As she herself was the daughter of a farm worker and had grown up in the countryside, she did not mind the seclusion and quietness of life in Drayton Beauchamp. The two married in 1962 and shortly afterwards moved into Painesend Farm Cottage which had by then been modernised and converted from two cottages into one. Because of the surprising number of small windows Peter and Sylvia named this cottage "Little Manse", a name which it kept for several years.

Peter knows this part of the parish intimately - its people, history and topography. He is able to pinpoint the position of the field called "Eldins" after which the converted Painesend barn has been named. (On the 1838 Tithe Map this seems to be the field called "Hilders".) This same field appeared in 1966 in one of the scenes in the film "The Specialist". This black and white comedy film, based on a book by Charles Sale, relates the exploits of a country carpenter, Lem Putt (played by Bernard Miles), who supposedly specialises in building superior privies. The film was shot during a two-week period around Painesend, Terriers End and Hang Hill, and local residents such as Peter and Archie West were used as film extras. Peter retains vivid memories of repeated "takes" of a scene in which the "newly-invented" privy erected by the filmmakers at the top of Eldins Field apparently tips over under the weight of several men who are seen following each other inside (but not seen quietly crawling out again at the back). More recently, this area was used as a location in the filming of "Land Girls" which also features the village church and its then Rector, the Reverend Alan Bennett.

Peter has been told that a blacksmith's shop used to be situated at the top of the field known as "Smith's Shop Field" between Hang Hill Cottages and Fiddlers Green. Great Hang Hill itself was, he has always believed, so named because of the hangings of outlaws which used to take place there in the days before turnpike roads were built and when travel through the Chilterns was exceedingly risky because of the number of brigands hiding in the dense woods. Authors such as Kelk and Sheahan are of the same opinion, but Keith Bailey, an expert in Buckinghamshire field names, disagrees, arguing that the field would in that case have been called "Gallows Hill" or "Gibbet Hill" instead. Bailey is sure that the Old English words "hangra" and "hangel" – meaning "wood on a steep hillside" or "a slope" - are the true origins of the name.

Peter is equally sure that the outline on the ground in Hang Hill Field which became visible during the dry summers of the mid 1970s and which some believe to be that of a Roman station has a much more prosaic explanation. Hay bales left in that field during this period became rotten and a farm worker known to Peter who was working for the contractor Frank Brown based at the top of the Crong was instructed to remove them. The tractor the man was using had a bad oil leak so that everywhere he drove the grass was killed by the oil and distinct marks about two feet apart and going off at various angles remained. The worker was eventually forced to leave the job unfinished because of the oil leak.

Peter and Sylvia have a daughter and a son. Both were born in the Royal Buckinghamshire Hospital but grew up, as did their father, in Hang Hill Cottages. Their daughter Elizabeth now lives in Hemel Hempstead and their son Richard in Aylesbury. In 2001, Peter and Sylvia retired and moved to Weston Turville. They are happy in their retirement and well settled in their bungalow.

Fiddlers Green

The oldest part of Fiddlers Green, a house of timber with brick infill construction, is believed to date from around 1640. The roof is also timber-framed and although now clay-tiled, may well have been thatched originally. The building has been extended outwards in both directions from its original core and it appears that a false brick frontage with two round windows (most unusual in a farm cottage) has been added at some time. A newer staircase has also been built and the original blocked up. A window which would have been on the outside wall of the house is now an internal one, and some of the old beams have been plastered over or painted white. The original house would have been a simple two up-two down dwelling with a barn nearby but the additions listed above would have turned it into a much more showy building. The rather grand brick surround to the large well in front of the house and the size of the garden add to this picture of Fiddlers Green as the home of a worker of some status. Examination by experts would, there is little doubt, yield fascinating detail to add to the little that is known. Unfortunately the deeds for the house are missing, seemingly lodged during the Second World War with the then owner's solicitor in Liverpool and destroyed during the bombing of that city.

In the 1838 Tithe Map and Apportionment Document the house, not named, was owned by the Jenney family. Shown as being divided into two tiny adjoining cottages, it was occupied by the families of George Jaycock and James Taylor, farm workers for the Jenney estate. James Taylor does not appear on the 1841 Census, but a young Eliza Taylor and her three small children are listed. All four have gone by the time of the next census.

It is interesting to discover that George Jaycock's wife Mary is named officially as having been in attendance at the death of Charles Choules, a "yeast manufacturer" of Painesend who died in 1845 from consumption. Even more intriguing is the fact that Ruth Jaycock, a relative by marriage, is named as having been present at the deaths of Samuel Cyster in 1858 and Ann Cyster in 1867. In many communities of the time, particular women would be used by villagers to attend the sick, dying, or those in labour. Perhaps, then, this was the role played by the Jaycock women in the upper part of the village.

In official records Fiddlers Green was traditionally included under the "Terriers End" heading, as were the two small adjoining cottages which used to stand next door to Terriers End. There seems little doubt, however, that generations of the extensive Jaycock family lived in one of the two "Fiddlers Green cottages" between 1838 and 1898, with members of the well-researched Cyster (or Syster) family followed by the Stevens family in the adjoining cottage. The Cysters had come to Drayton Beauchamp by the end of the 18th century and seem always to have lived in one of the cottages around Painesend Farm. A Jenney Estate document of 1898 finally and reliably identifies Fiddlers Green as "Keeper's Cottage", part of

Painesend Farm and occupied by John Lovegrove.

Frank Harrowell of Tring (1900-1985), writing some 60 years ago about his memories of this part of the parish and the people who lived in each cottage, recalled that Fiddlers Green was indeed used by Stewart William Jenney to house his gamekeeper, John Lovegrove. John's first wife Ruth (née Gurney) of Tring whom he married in 1866 died in late 1882 aged 37. The following year he married Eliza Payne and the family moved to Drayton Beauchamp. John and Eliza had two children. In the 1891 Census John, his wife Eliza, seven children (the oldest five from John's first marriage), and Eliza's widowed mother Amelia Payne are named as occupants at Fiddlers Green, suggesting that the house was no longer being used as two cottages for two separate families. Interestingly, John's grandfather Joseph had married a Drayton Beauchamp woman "Phillis" Bridges in 1804 and his uncle Joseph had married another Drayton Beauchamp woman, Eliza Flaxman or Flexman, in 1849, so although the Lovegrove family were based mainly in Buckland and Aston Clinton, they had long-standing connections with Drayton Beauchamp – as indeed had the Gurney family. In the 1841 Census Joseph Lovegrove's future wife Eliza Flaxman, aged 12, is listed as living in the Dower House along with Henry and Ann Foskett, thus demonstrating that the upper and lower ends of the parish shared family ties and probably felt less separate from each other than they do today. Coincidentally, a Thomas Flaxman of Drayton Beauchamp was given exemption in 1812 from serving in the Cottesloe Hundreds Militia for men 18-45 because of medical problems, but it has not so far been possible to discover whether or not he was a relative of Eliza.

John Lovegrove died in February 1905. Five months later, John's son Walter, a soldier, married his cousin Emily Hedges. Emily was a daughter of John Hedges who had married Sarah Lovegrove, John Lovegrove's sister. Emily's brother, Frank John, was killed in 1917 at Vimy Ridge aged 25. Frank John had emigrated to Ontario in 1912 and enlisted only one week after marrying in 1915. Emily's nephew, Frank James, died as a child after being knocked down by a motorcycle, and one of her nieces was Dorothy Primrose (Peggy) who later became Peggy Elvy, a well-known figure in Drayton Beauchamp until her death in 1994. In this way, as often happened in the Drayton Beauchamp of the past, two large families intermarried in one generation after another. Indeed a strong link through marriage also existed between the Lovegrove and Ball families.

Two of John Lovegrove's sons, Frederick and Edward, served in the Oxfordshire and Buckinghamshire Light Infantry during World War I but must have survived as they are listed again at Fiddlers Green in the Electoral Registers of 1919 and 1920. Sadly, at least four of John's children died in early childhood, two of them little girls aged six and four who died within twelve days of each other – perhaps the two diphtheria fatalities recorded in the London Daily News of 31st October 1891. A further two of John's children died in particularly tragic circumstances. Frank Harrowell talks of a Lovegrove son dying during the 1918 flu epidemic and a daughter "dying of shock" upon coming into the house and seeing her dead brother. In the village church's Burial Records, William Lovegrove aged 34 is recorded as dying on 9th November 1918 and his sister Edith Annie (24) on the same day. Both death certificates list the probable cause of death as "syncope following influenza and chronic heart disease." It can readily be imagined, then, that the young woman, already weakened by influenza and with a long-standing cardiac disorder, collapsed and died on the same day as her brother. Their mother Eliza registered the deaths, signing with a cross.

In 1919 Major Jenney sold Fiddlers Green at the same time as he sold many of his village properties but Eliza Lovegrove stayed on as tenant until 1928 when the house was sold again. She died in 1940 aged 86. The new owner in 1928 was Melville Jamieson, a Canadian, who asked Frank Harrowell to attach to a wall inside the house "a piece of oak panelling with historic value". This panel is still in place exactly as Frank described.

It is not until as recently as 1935 that the name Fiddlers Green first appears on Electoral Registers. It is not known why this particular name was chosen for the house, but the expression apparently refers to an imagined afterlife like the Elysian Fields where, according to Wikipedia, "there is perfect mirth, a fiddle that never stops playing, and dancers who never tire." It appears in both military and naval songs and in poems in various countries. It has been suggested – perhaps because of the connotations of the name – that Fiddlers Green served in the past as a public house, but this seems highly unlikely given its isolated nature and the fact that it has no cellar for storing alcohol.

Phil and Hilary Hurst

In April 2010 Fiddlers Green, now a substantial house with five bedrooms, three large public rooms and a sizeable barn all sitting on around an acre of land, was bought by Phil and Hilary Hurst. Phil originates from Bushey Heath; Hilary was born in Amersham but moved as a toddler to Wilstone. The couple's first home was in Chipperfield near Watford. Six years later they moved to an old cottage in a rural setting near the canal on the edge of Tring and stayed there for thirteen years. Looking for more space and a friendly rural community which would still be within reasonable reach of schools and main line stations, Fiddlers Green has proved to be their ideal home in the ideal location – the perfect place to bring up their son, born in 1999, and their daughter, born in 2001. Both children attend school locally. Phil works in London as a civil and structural engineer while Hilary's training is in medical writing.

The family have settled quickly and very happily in their new home and cannot envisage ever wanting to move elsewhere although they are sure that in time they will want to do exploratory work in the house to uncover some of the features which have been blocked up over the years – old beams, doorways and a fireplace, for instance. They have made friends locally – but with others living in the three valleys which come together near Fiddlers Green rather than in the "main village" of Drayton Beauchamp nearer to the church. Hilary makes a point of driving through the lower part of the village regularly so as to maintain some feeling of connection with it. So far, however, she and Phil feel that they have not been able to build up a picture of who lives where and what may be going on in the village. This sense of dislocation is heightened by various factors - the couple's newness to the area, for instance, and the lack until very recently of a village newsletter. In addition, the distance of Fiddlers Green from the main concentration of houses in the parish, the artificial boundaries created by the A41 bypass and the Upper Icknield Way, and the fact that Fiddlers Green seems to be claimed by both Buckinghamshire and Hertfordshire, all contribute to the idiosyncratic difficulties which face newcomers to this part of the village.

DRAYTON MANOR

BROADVIEW FARM   Paul & Elaine Slough & Family

THE MOAT HOUSE 1970

Oakengrove

For at least 175 years buildings of some kind – a farmhouse and barns, a cottage or pair of cottages – have stood on or in close proximity to the same site at the southern extremity of Drayton Beauchamp parish on Shire Lane, the name of the building(s) changing from Oakengrove to Oak Grove and back again. It is documented in old records that Lucy Manners, the then lord of the manor of Drayton Beauchamp, bought Oakengrove – a "messuage plus twenty-three acres of land" shortly before she died in 1835, although the identity of the previous owner has not so far been discovered.

In the Tithe Map and accompanying Apportionment Document of 1838, Oakengrove and 63 acres of land are shown as being owned by William Christopher/Jenney and occupied by James Bull, a saddler. A decade later James's son George is listed there as both farmer and brick maker. George's wife Rosetta died in March 1861 aged 31, during or soon after the birth of the couple's seventh child and after little more than ten years of marriage. In the census of that year (taken on 7th April) a nurse is listed as one of the residents of Oakengrove, employed no doubt to help care for the Bulls' seven children who ranged in age from eight years down to the three-week-old baby. Kelly's Directories until 1869 name George Bull as farmer and brickmaker at Oakengrove but in each of the four censuses thereafter a different tenant is named at Oakengrove. In 1872 a fourteen-year lease was agreed with Frederick Crouch of Tring.

By 1898 Oakengrove was being rented to Lord Rothschild, and was said to consist of a house of seven rooms along with an open shed, barn, cowshed and poultry house and just over 64 acres. The rent was £64 per annum. In 1907 a cottage at Oakengrove was demolished. In May 1911 Oakengrove, another small cottage nearby, and the farm lands and woods around were sold by Stewart William Jenney to Nathaniel ("Natty") Rothschild, the first Baron Rothschild, for £4523 1s 2d, a price which was agreed upon only after lengthy and rather angry negotiations. The following year the farmhouse was pulled down, the last tenant listed being James Largen, an estate carpenter, who was living there with his wife and fifteen-year-old daughter, described as a dressmaker. Lodging with the Largen family was Arthur Holland, a groom of shire horses. In the cottage nearby – also soon to be pulled down - were Arthur Corbett, a forester, his wife Nellie and their small child. In 1913 (the date being carved in the beam over the door) a new building, divided into two cottages and called Oakengrove Cottages, was erected to house workers on the Rothschild estate. The construction of this new Oakengrove was part of Nathaniel Rothschild's project to demolish old buildings in Hastoe and to redevelop them in the style he liked. New farm buildings, a Working Men's Club, a chapel and labourers' cottages were built by Lord Rothschild for his wife Emma who would visit her "model village" in a trap pulled by a Grevy's zebra. Local children tried to guess the route she would take in the hope of being rewarded with a sixpence if they opened the appropriate gates.

The 1915 Valuation Book identifies James Largen and Nathan Brackley as the tenants of the "new house at Oakengrove" owned by Lord Rothschild. Nathaniel Rothschild died in 1915, Emma in 1935, and their son Walter, 2nd Baron Rothschild, in 1937. Their grandson Victor Rothschild, 3rd Baron Rothschild, then put most of the Tring Park Estate up for auction by Horwood and James on 31st October 1938 at the Rose and Crown in Tring. A number of properties were, however, sold privately prior to the auction. Among these were the two adjoining Oakengrove cottages which were bought in March 1938 by Joseph Timberlake, manager of Hastoe Farm and its tenant from 1915. Joseph Timberlake bought Hastoe and Longcroft Farms outright in 1938, living at Hastoe Farm until he died in 1942. His son Kenneth Jack Timberlake sold the right-hand Oakengrove cottage as viewed from the lane (known as 226 Shire Lane) to William Russell in May 1959 and the left-hand cottage (225 Shire Lane) in March 1961. In 1960 Kenneth Timberlake sold at auction both Longcroft and Hastoe Farms.

Roger and Elaine Wellby

In early 1961, Oakengrove, which still consisted of 2 two-storey cottages with separate staircases, was bought from William Russell by Rear-Admiral Roger Wellby and his wife Elaine who had returned to England from Melbourne, Australia. Roger and Elaine had met and married in Alexandria where Elaine's father, Sir Clifford Heathcote-Smith, was Consul General for fifteen years. Retiring after a career in the Royal Navy, Roger wanted to live as far as possible from the sea and Oakengrove met this condition, both horizontally and vertically, as well as providing the cold, strong winds he had for so long been used to on the bridge of his ship. He had relatives living in Berkhamsted, and the couple's two younger sons – sixteen and thirteen when they moved to Oakengrove – attended school in Berkhamsted, cycling the seven miles each way every day. (The oldest boy, nineteen, remained in Melbourne at university.)

In 1961 there were still barns and a well which were all much older than the house, but the barns (one a lovely old wooden barn with a hay loft) were burned down – along with others in the area - by a man angry that his brother had been sent to prison. A depression in the field behind the house remains as evidence of the German V-bomb which fell on 16th August 1944, damaging the crops and the roof of the house. The roof was repaired with tiles of a lighter colour than the rest. The Wellbys did a great deal to upgrade and modernise Oakengrove which, by the time they left in 1995, was a substantial house of five bedrooms and four public rooms. The grounds of around 1½ acres which originally went with Oakengrove were extended when Roger bought a five-acre field and then a four-acre wood (a wood which may have given Oakengrove its name in the first place).

Roger and Elaine Wellby loved Oakengrove, their "home among the summer pastures in the high hills" and they remained hospitable, active and full of mischievous fun even when very elderly. They had a huge circle of friends and were involved in many local and national organisations. They enjoyed country pursuits and sports and encouraged a spirit of adventure in their sons and other young visitors. The whole family attended the village church regularly and loved the beautiful setting of the church in the meadows. They were not involved in village activities beyond the church, however, and felt socially more attached to Berkhamsted than to Drayton Beauchamp.

In 1995, Elaine and Roger moved to Wendover, no longer able to cope with the garden and land at Oakengrove, but reluctant to leave the house in which they had been so happy for so long. Roger died in 2003 aged 97 and Elaine in 2005 aged 91. The two had been happily married for 67 years. Both are buried in Drayton Beauchamp churchyard, their grave marked by a headstone with a hare engraved on it to recall their many years of beagling – a pursuit they continued to enjoy several times a week even when they were in their eighties.

Martin and Patsy Tye

Martin, who originates from Bushey in Hertfordshire, and Patsy who comes from Ireland, moved from London to Oakengrove in 1995, buying from the Wellbys the house, barn, stables and eight acres which included a paddock and woods. In recent months the couple have undertaken a major renovation of the house.

Since living at Oakengrove Martin and Patsy have had three sons, all born at Oakengrove and now aged twelve, ten and eight (Harvey, Roddy and Oskar respectively); all attend school in Amersham. Martin owns a business which makes and supplies stainless steel worktops, cabinets, and so on. Patsy looks after the home and children.

Martin and Patsy were attracted to Oakengrove because of its rural setting and the accessibility of good horse-riding country. Although on paper Oakengrove falls within the boundaries of the parish of Drayton Beauchamp the couple are closer geographically to Hastoe and Cholesbury and their friends are drawn from a wide area.

Rye Hill Farm

The 31 acres of arable land (appropriately named Rye Hill) on part of which Rye Hill Farm now stands is listed in the 1838 Tithe Map and Apportionment Document as being part of the estate of William Christopher/Jenney of Drayton Manor. The tenant in 1838 was Thomas Griffin who was farming just over 154 acres in and around the village from his base as tenant farmer at Upper Farm. The first mention found so far of a property called Rye Hill Farm is in the Electoral Register of 1933. The original Rye Hill Farm is believed to have been a smallholding of a little over two acres of land with a tiny farm cottage – a brick building with a tiled roof. No foundations were deemed necessary as the house was built on boulder chalk. For the first thirteen years the Electoral Registers list a succession of different residents, many staying for only two or three years.

The Ballad Family

In 1946/7 Marion and Gordon Ballad moved with their daughter and baby son David from Aylesbury to Rye Hill Farm. A second daughter was born several years later.

David Ballad's whole childhood was spent at Rye Hill Farm and he moved away only when he married in 1968. David is a member of the Ballad family who were well-known and respected members of the Drayton Beauchamp community for many years. Throughout David's childhood, his uncle Fred and his aunts Edie and Florrie owned Lower Farm. Florrie Ballad's photograph album documents the village as she knew it in the first half of the twentieth century, capturing notable events such as the heavy snowfall of 1926 which blocked the village lane for three days and the severe thunderstorm of 30th April 1929 which felled an ash tree and caused other damage in the village. David himself remembers the winter of 1962 when deep snowdrifts lay until March. On one occasion he had to use the tractor to tow out Mrs Oliphant in her car which had become stuck in the deep snow near the village bridge.

David's parents both worked in a bank in Aylesbury but came to Drayton Beauchamp because of a wish to take up farming. Gordon, and David too from a young age, not only farmed their own land, but helped other farmers in the village as well. David recalls that he helped Gladys Chapman at Church Hill Farm hand-milk her Jersey cows before he went to school and that she was tossed and badly hurt by one of her bulls. His father was himself kicked by a cow and his arm fractured. David worked alongside William Sanders at Broadview Farm and remembers an ancient airfield tractor being used there with a modified engine and small wheels to increase the speed. Indeed, tractors were an important part of life for David and his father. David learned to drive a tractor when he was no more than eight years old and his father never owned a car, using instead a David

Brown Cropmaster tractor as his sole form of transport. The tractor-drawn thrashing machine used by David's father in fields he had beyond the B489 on the way to Puttenham was the last to be used in the area. As a very small child, David remembers the thrashing machine being pushed and pulled through the entrance to the yard at Rye Hill Farm for use in the fields there too.

As a child, David's closest village friends were Richard Gregory and Mick Anns. Playing cricket was an activity enjoyed by all three. David would provide the cricket bat and stumps and Mick would mow the "cricket pitch" in the field where Kimego and Treasures now sit. A pair of furry gauntlets served as cricket gloves. The moats provided opportunities for fishing and for adventures in the punt which was moored there, although even as a boy David's farming duties left him with little time to play. On Sunday mornings he pumped the organ (then situated in the choir) in the village church and he enjoyed social events such as the Christmas Play in the schoolhouse. He attended primary school in Aston Clinton and secondary school in Aylesbury.

David remembers many villagers – the Menday family next door at Ryecote with boys John and Bob, and Sid, David and Val Lake at Bridge Farm. The Walls lived at The Close and Harry Nicholls at Upper Farm. Coming down through the village, he recalls the Hicks family in one of the cottages now known as Badgers End and the Stillwells in the other (Mr Stillwell being a Lieutenant in the Royal Navy). There were no houses between the Homestead and Badgers End (where Applewood, Kimego and Treasures now stand), that area of land being a very boggy water meadow – as well as being the village boys' favourite place for cricket.

Alan and Esmé Southam lived in Drayton Cottage, Wally and Ethel Kempster in Sunnyside, the Reynolds and then the Misses Dewick in the Dower House, and Peggy Elvy in Beauchamp Cottages with her parents across the lane at Ballad Cottages (later called the Homestead and now Setherwood). Mick Hannon and his family lived in one of the Upper Farm Cottages and the Gregory family in the other. The Oliphants were at Morgans Farm and the Scotts at the Rectory before moving to Lower Farm in 1960.

David left school when he was fifteen and cycled every day to work in Wendover where he drove the combine harvester on a farm along the Ellesborough Road. One year later during the winter of 1962/3 he began work at Morgans Farm milking the cows for Bill Oliphant. During his working life he has lived in several different places but most of his work has been of a farming nature and much of it with cows, so he is used to wakening at 4.30 a.m. and managing with little sleep. In 1968 he married Brenda who comes from Tring and whom he met when she was a schoolgirl working on Saturdays at Atkins the bakers in Tring. They have two adult sons and now live in a farm cottage at Ringshall where David continued to milk cows until the last of the herd was sold. He recently retired from work at

Ashridge Management College.

David's parents remained in the village until 1970 when they sold Rye Hill Farm for £4500 and moved to Aylesbury. By this time his father had reluctantly concluded that farming was no longer economically viable and had become a Traffic Warden in Aylesbury until ill health forced him to retire. His parents then moved to Kettering where his father died several years ago. His mother still lives there. A link with the village remains, however, in that David's uncles (his father's brothers) Joe and John still own land between the B489 and the bridge at Puttenham.

David considers Drayton Beauchamp a beautiful village and remembers many happy times during the 22 years he lived at Rye Hill Farm.

James Loosley

James and Vivien Loosley, both of whom originate from within ten miles of Drayton Beauchamp, married in 1966 and had two daughters. They were planning to extend their house in Tring when Rye Hill Farm came on to the market in 1982. They took up residence that year and in 1994 bought just over three acres of land from Don and Margaret Hunt of Drayton Holloway (a further part of the field called "Upper Rye Hill" in the 1838 Tithe Map), thereby increasing their acreage to a total of between six and seven acres. In 1971 the then owners of Rye Hill Farm successfully applied to open livery stables there and Vivien Loosley continued to use the land for horses until 1997 when the Loosleys' marriage ended and Rye Hill Farm was again sold.

James, an accountant by profession, now lives in Aston Clinton with his second wife. James looks back on Drayton Beauchamp as a village divided by the bridge near the church. Some links were made across the divide, but in general those whose homes lay between the bridge and the Upper Icknield Way were, he believes, not considered to be living in the "village proper".

The current owners of Rye Hill Farm have bought a further area of land adjoining the Upper Icknield Way where mink used to be farmed. Over the years many extensions have been added to Rye Hill Farm so the house itself is now a substantial two-storey dwelling surrounded by several stables and barns.

Ryecote

In the 1838 Tithe Map and the Apportionment Document which accompanies it, all of the land along the left side of the Hollow Way stretching uphill from the Wendover Arm of the Grand Union Canal and finishing at the Upper Icknield Way was owned by William Christopher/Jenney of Drayton Manor. The area in which the house Ryecote now stands straddles the 1838 boundaries of two fields tenanted by John Parrott (at that time tenant farmer of a substantial estate comprising Morgans Farm, Lower Farm, and more than 476 acres) and Thomas Griffin (tenant farmer of Upper Farm and 154 acres). These fields were called Rye Hill and Upper Rye Hill.

It had been believed that three derelict wattle and daub dwellings with earth closets and thatched roofs may once have sat on this land. On maps dating back as far as 1736, however, no buildings of any kind are depicted between Upper Farm and the Upper Icknield Way and the land is described as arable fields. Only in the late 1920s/early 1930s were two small bungalows, of special bricks - "grey browns" - made by H.G. Matthews of Bellingdon, constructed in the fields alongside the Holloway between the canal and the Upper Icknield Way. One was named Ryecote and the other Rye Hill Farm.

Ryecote first appears on Electoral Registers by that name only in 1935 although a resident with the same surname is listed the previous year at Rye Hill. The owners of Ryecote for almost thirty years until 1974 were Florence and Jack Menday. Jack worked on local farms until he retired and the couple moved to Aylesbury. Both are buried in the village churchyard.

The house originally stood in an acre of land, but at some point before 1974 half of this land was sold to the then owners of Rye Hill Farm.

The current owner and his wife moved into Ryecote in 1974, having first made improvements including the replacement of the toilet which previously could be reached only by walking round the outside of the house. Ryecote now has three bedrooms and two public rooms.

The Close

It seems virtually certain that The Close, a house name which first appears on parish Electoral Registers in 1938, is the same house as was previously known as The Wayside. Ruth Akerman, born in the village in 1920, remembers clearly that the first owners in 1931/2, Edward and Elizabeth Kazer, and the second owner, Elsie Poole, called the house "The Wayside". In 1935 the house was bought by Elsa Christmas who changed the name to The Close three years later.

The significance of the name is that it may well mark the location of the sheep close in which the animals would have been kept during the winter. Brought down the holloway from the pastures at the upper extremity of the parish around Painesend Farm, they would have overwintered in what is a sheltered U-shaped valley with a bank on three sides, close to the main settlement but easily moved back to the summer pastures once winter was over.

The land on which The Close now sits was called Damwell Close in the 1838 Tithe Map and Apportionment Document, and was classified as arable land. It was owned by William Christopher/Jenney and rented to John Parrott. Part of the land which now extends to almost two acres was in the past a medieval ridge and furrow field, the outline of one step still visible on the hillside. The soil changes from chalk to clay halfway down the hill.

Until 1978 there were two sets of deeds – one for the house and garden, the other for the landlocked "Damwell Close". The deeds have now been amalgamated into one document. Next door was a car bodywork repair business – "Drayton Motors" – on a quarter acre of land owned by the previous residents of The Close and rented out. It was then sold to a developer but the building later burned down, and the current owners of The Close were finally able to buy the land on which it had sat.

The house itself is a bungalow with two bedrooms, and is believed to have been built from materials taken from Army/RAF buildings when they were demolished (including the heavy panelled internal doors thought to be of Columbian pine). The original red roof tiles were fitted diagonally in a pattern seen in houses in several nearby villages, and the external walls consist of a wooden frame which has been rendered.

Bob and Linda Rollason

In 1978 Bob and Linda Rollason bought The Close, moving there from Stevenage. Bob comes originally from Birmingham and Linda, born in the east end of London, was brought up in Stevenage. They met in Welwyn Garden City where both were working for a company which conducted research into rubber products for the Malaysian Rubber Fund Board - Bob as a senior scientist and Linda as a lab technician - and married in 1972. Eventually Bob's work involved travelling to several widely-spread places and Drayton Beauchamp proved to be a convenient location from where he could commute to all of them, while The Close had the land needed for the competition horses which Linda trained. Subsequently she bred and showed golden retrievers and is still a member of the Kennel Club and of the British Association of Professional Dog Trainers. For the past twenty years she and Bob have raised rare breed sheep instead (including Wiltshire Horns which moult rather than needing to be sheared) – thus returning the land to its original use.

Bob and Linda have found that Drayton Beauchamp lacks the usual "feel" of a village. Drayton Bridge seems to act as a dividing line between what are in effect two villages, with the Upper and Lower Icknield Way adding to the problem by cutting off the two farthest extremities of the village. There is no "social centre" such as a pub or village hall and there are never sufficient residents of any one age group or shared interest to have a common reason to meet together. The cost of buying a house in the village is too high for most first-time buyers or those with small children, so the village population is likely to become increasingly an ageing one, with few young people living here and able to breathe new life into it. Even so, Linda and Bob are happy to remain here and would leave only if physically no longer able to meet the challenges of living in this rather isolated village or to continue with the work involved in running the smallholding.

THE CLOSE

Bob & Linda Rollason

BROADVIEW HOUSE

Anne & Derrick Ball

CHURCH HILL FARM

Bob & Janet Smith

Broadview Farm

William and Kathleen Sanders

In April 1959, William (Bill) and Kathleen (Kay) Sanders and their son Roger, then ten, and daughter Moira, then six, moved from Stoke Mandeville to 22 acres of land in Drayton Beauchamp which they had bought from a Mr John Brown who farmed beef, arable and pigs with his son at Wendover and who had owned a small plot of land in Drayton Beauchamp since before the War. The land had not previously been a farm in its own right, but in the 1838 Tithe Map and accompanying Apportionment Document it is listed as part of Rye Hill. The Sanders established a dairy and arable farm from scratch on this land with 21 cows (a mixture of Guernsey, Jersey, Friesian, Ayrshire and Shorthorn breeds). In addition to the 22 acres, the family rented a ten-acre field to the east of their land and a further twenty acres lower down the village. Roger and his father used to walk the heifers to and from these fields along the lane through the village.

Bill Sanders was a Crop Inspector with Elsoms Seeds of Spalding at that time, having trained at the Royal College of Agriculture, Cirencester. He came originally from Essex where he had won the Essex County Show Pig Prize two years running in 1951 and 1952.

A barn already on the land contained a large array of farm machinery, some dating from before World War II, including a Massey Ferguson tractor and, in particular, a 1923 Fordson tractor. Bill's love of machinery and his five years with the Royal Tank Regiment in the War meant that all items were working within a matter of weeks.

One field to the south marked the parish boundary between Drayton Beauchamp and Drayton Holloway, while a stream at the eastern edge of the plot marked the Buckinghamshire and Hertfordshire boundary. The Sanders children clearly recall enjoying games of "jumping from one county to the other" over the stream. A public footpath ran through the middle of the land going up to the Upper Icknield Way to the south. The breathtaking views of the Vale of Aylesbury to the north from a height of five hundred feet gave rise to the name "Broadview Farm" as the land had had no name previously. The excellent position of the fields meant that the family always had a "ringside view" of the annual Battle of Britain air display at nearby RAF Halton each September and saw the first Comet land there in 1959.

At the insistence of Barclay's Bank, and remembering similar buildings they had seen when living in Canada, the Sanders bought a single storey cedar shingle bungalow made by Colt, a firm based in Tenterden, Kent, and had it erected as their farmhouse by Alan Hicks, a Tring builder. The couple had a road built to the farm from the Holloway, installing telephone and electricity cables and a water supply.   While the construction was under way during the long hot summer of 1959 (the warmest of the twentieth century until 1976) the family lived on site in a brand new building which eventually was to become the chicken house! Roger recalls celebrating his tenth birthday in September 1959 in the "chicken shed" but being in his new bedroom in the bungalow by the time of the General Election in October of that year.

The family grew barley as well as keeping the dairy herd, buying and selling cows in Aylesbury Cattle Market, and rearing chickens and rabbits. Their neighbours were Gladys Chapman of Church Hill Farm who owned all of the land between her farmhouse and the B488 on the west side of the Holloway, and the Ballad family who lived at Rye Hill Farm. For a while in 1961, Bill helped Miss Chapman by milking her cows morning and evening (as well as his own) whilst she was without a farm manager.

In 1962 the family decided that they needed a larger farm with more cows than the 22 acres of Broadview Farm could support and sold to Bill Moorhouse. Bill already lived in Drayton Beauchamp and now turned Broadview Farm into a pig farm. The Sanders family moved in May 1962 to Northdown Farm in the village of Merton, near Great Torrington in Devon, with views of both Exmoor and Dartmoor and land overlooking the River Torridge - just in time to be cut off for three weeks by the snowdrifts of the Big Freeze in the long winter of 1962/63.

Bill Sanders died in December 2004 at the age of 80; Kay died in January 2010, aged 86. They are buried together in the public cemetery at Wroxham, Norfolk.

The Moorhouse Family

Between 1962 and 1977 the Broadview Farm bungalow was owned by the Moorhouses and was often used to accommodate the farm's pig managers. Karen Moorhouse lived there with her new husband Norman Brown for a time too. In 1977 the farm bungalow was sold to Elaine and Paul Slough.

Paul and Elaine Slough

Elaine Slough comes from Lincolnshire while her husband, Paul, was brought up by his grandparents who farmed in Bedfordshire. Paul and Elaine met through the MG Car Club in 1963, marrying a year later. They lived first in Barnet, Hertfordshire, and then in Essendon, also in Hertfordshire, where they renovated two derelict cottages and converted them into one house. Elaine is by profession a graphic designer. Paul spent most of his working life in the car industry, both in the workshop and in sales, as well as having an international rally licence.

For several years after moving to Broadview Farm in 1977, Paul continued to work in the motor industry at the same time as running the farm where he and Elaine kept pigs until 1982 and later on cattle until 2008, renting land in the surrounding countryside to supplement the ten acres which now goes along with Broadview Farm. They remember with amusement the jumping abilities of the Limousin cross cattle who could clear a five barred gate with apparent ease.

Since 1977 Elaine and Paul have done a great deal to upgrade Broadview Farm, doubling the size of the rooms. (There are three bedrooms and two public rooms, all now of generous proportions.) The couple have a son and daughter. Their son lives in Portugal; their daughter, a graphic designer with her own business, lives with them and is very involved with horses which she breaks and trains for eventing – horses bred by Elaine who has many years of such experience.

Paul and Elaine like the village as it is and have always found other villagers friendly. They keep in close contact with the other farmers in the area, offering each other support and alerting each other to emergencies such as the theft of farm equipment. Their two regrets are the speed at which some vehicles drive along the Holloway and the litter thrown or "fly-tipped" regularly from passing vehicles. They cannot envisage ever moving elsewhere and intend to stay here for the rest of their lives.

Broadview House

William and Sheila Moorhouse

Broadview House with its twelve acres of land was built in 1971 in the field identified in the 1838 Tithe Map as Rye Hill, and was the first building to be erected on that particular site. The construction was commissioned by Bill Moorhouse who moved there with his family after living for nine years at the Moat House near the village church. Broadview House and the nearby one-storey farmhouse bungalow which Bill had bought from Bill Sanders in 1962 originally sat in a total of around forty acres of land on which more than 1000 pigs were reared. Bill specialised in producing a prize-winning cross-breed from the long-backed Landrace pig and the Large White. His herdsman was Jim Anns whom he had originally employed at his Sunglow Factory in Aylesbury and then at the Moat House as his gardener.

Karen Moorhouse, daughter of Bill and Sheila, married in 1975 and lived for a time with her husband Norman Brown at the bungalow next door before moving to Aylesbury. The couple now live in a rural part of Devon. Bill and Sheila sold Broadview House and Broadview Farm in 1979, moving to Weston Turville and opening a gift shop, Magpies, in Tring. The final move of this enterprising couple was to Tenerife. Both died a few years ago.

Derrick and Anne Ball

Derrick and Anne Ball, who both originate from London, moved to Tring around 1966 and bought Broadview House on 15th June, 1979. They had a son (then fifteen) and a daughter (then thirteen). Their daughter was a keen horsewoman who was now able to keep her horse on the family's land. For some time Anne became the resident farmer, combining this with her work at Stoke Mandeville Hospital, while Derrick divided his time between his work as a freelance tax consultant in London and taking courses at Hampden Hall Farming College in Stoke Mandeville where he learned about pig, sheep and cattle rearing, welding and so on. Over the years the couple have kept a wide variety of animals and birds – among them sheep, calves, chickens and ducks. They have had no livestock for ten years although the property is still registered as a farm holding.

The Balls have made only minor changes to Broadview House since 1979 and have no plans currently for changes to the house or to their lifestyle. They look back on their years as farmers with pleasure, and have particularly happy memories of the social aspects of farming activities at that time. Their one regret is that, lacking a focal point such as a shop or hall, there is no natural village meeting point for residents of Drayton Beauchamp and much of the Balls' socialising is still carried out in Tring where they have friends of many years' standing.

Church Hill Farm

Situated right beside "Dan'l's Corner" (a spot feared by villagers of times gone by because of their conviction that ghosts including a headless horseman in livery used to pace there on dark nights), Church Hill Farm was built around 1935. There seems not to have been a building on the site before this, but the area is identified on the 1838 Tithe Map and Apportionment Document as glebe land owned by the church in the person of the Rev. Thomas Naylor Bland, Rector of Drayton Beauchamp. Called "Picked Close", this arable land extended to just over three acres, and was rented by John Parrott. The current land which goes with the property must have included also the lowest section of what was in 1838 called Church Hill field, an arable field of 36 acres farmed by Thomas Griffin.

As with many other village properties, Church Hill Farm seems to have started off as a smallholding. For instance Gladys Chapman, the owner from 1947 until 1964, kept a few Jersey cattle and bred Mexican Chihuahuas. (Gladys's father had been cowman in charge of a pedigree Jersey herd on the Rothschild Estate). Roger Sanders, whose father established Broadview Farm in 1959, can remember his father helping to milk the cows at Church Hill Farm when Gladys Chapman was without a farm manager. David Ballad of Rye Hill Farm also remembers hand-milking Gladys's cows in the mornings before he went to school. A horrible accident, still remembered, was when one of her bulls attacked her, causing her serious injuries. A large barn stood near the farmhouse and village children used to hurry past holding their noses to escape the pungent smell of cattle manure.

Originally a small brick-built cottage, Church Hill Farm was extended by the Fitzpatricks who bought the property after Gladys Chapman died. Kevin and Pat Fitzpatrick lived there from 1965 until 1985 and Pat ran a children's nursery/playgroup there. The house has been extended again by the current owners and now consists of five bedrooms, two public rooms and a large family kitchen. The rear of the house looks down over the church, canal, and lower part of the village. There are eight acres which include two fields – one to the side of the house and the other running down towards the canal. These fields are planted and harvested by Bill Rawdings, son-in-law of Pat Moss, the rally driver. The field which stretches up alongside the Holloway to its junction with the Upper Icknield Way also belongs to Bill and was said by Wally Kempster of Sunnyside to have been used many years ago for the growing of lavender.

Bob and Janet Smith

Bob Smith was born in Hemel Hempstead but was brought up in Tring; his wife Janet comes from Mill Hill but moved with her family to Tring as a teenager. After marrying, the couple moved to Wendover and in 1986 sold their house there. They learned from Stan Ward (whose widow Evelyn still lives at 1 Church Lane) that Church Hill Farm was for sale, and purchased it although they were aware that an intrusive bypass to Aston Clinton might possibly be constructed at some future time.

Sadly, the bypass, now built, has had a damaging effect on the tranquillity of their environment. It has encroached on their land, closed off old walks they used to enjoy, and changed their outlook because of the many trees which were felled during the construction process. The couple regret too the speed at which drivers try to negotiate the dangerous corner in front of Church Hill Farm and the frequency with which rubbish is dumped at the top of the Holloway.

Because of the distance of Church Hill Farm from the main group of houses in the lower part of the village, Bob and Janet feel very separate from the village, and do not even know their nearer neighbours well. They regret that there is no central point where villagers could meet and note that even although they have lived here for 25 years, their friends still tend to be those they have made outside the village. Their two adult sons, however, both live nearby in Tring and are fully involved with the family business of wall and floor tiling. Janet herself still does all of the bookkeeping for the business.

The couple have no plans to leave Drayton Beauchamp and would find it very hard to give up the open spaces and the freedom of living in such a tiny village, especially as they enjoy keeping several dogs. They recognise, however, that at some point the house may become too much for them to manage.

Bridge Farm and Orchard Croft

The land on which Bridge Farm used to stand, and where Orchard Croft is now situated, belonged originally to the Jenney family of Drayton Manor, and is listed in the 1838 Tithe Map and Apportionment Document as being a thirty-acre arable field called Pyes Hill whose tenant at that time was John Parrott. An old photograph which has come to light shows a Fordson Model F tractor dating from between 1917 and 1922 pulling a plough across what is almost certainly Pyes Hill with the canal and village bridge in the background. This field appears again in a catalogue advertising the sale by auction of the Morgans Farm estate on 5th July 1926. Here it is described as "an enclosure of land in lucerne, pasture and grass seeds". The purchaser in 1926 is not known, but it may well have been Fred Green, a World War I veteran living in Buckland, who by the autumn of 1931 had constructed a bungalow on this land for himself and his wife Winifred. Johnnie, their son, was friend and ally in mischief to Mick Anns who still lives in the village.

By 1937 Fred Green had sold five of the thirty acres to Bernard and Violet Banfield who built the house called "Greenpath" (later renamed Rye House) on it. The remaining 25 acres of land extend from the Holloway parallel to the Wendover Arm of the Grand Union Canal and close to the village bridge from which the farm took its name.

In May 1958 Sidney Lake bought Bridge Farm from the Greens who retired to Tring although Fred continued to work the land he was renting at Drayton Manor. Sidney Lake had himself been farming at Heath End near Cholesbury with his brother, and by coincidence their land there ran adjacent to the fields of Vale Farm, home of Harry Nicholls before he came to Drayton Beauchamp in 1948 to take over Upper Farm. Both Heath End and Vale Farm were part of the Rossway estate. Sidney remained at Bridge Farm until his death in 1991, and is buried in the village churchyard.

David and Valerie Lake

Sidney's son David came to the village in 1958 as a teenager with the rest of his family, and trained as a bricklayer. His work took him to many towns and cities, and in the 1960s he was involved in the construction of Bedgrove as a new and very large estate. In 1962 David married Valerie, a Cholesbury girl who worked as a hairdresser in Amersham. The two lived in a caravan at the farm while they waited for approval to build a bungalow in what had been the orchard of Bridge Farm. The new chalet bungalow had been completed by 1967 and was called Orchard Croft. Sidney Lake kept milking cattle until he retired around 1974 and handed over the running of Bridge Farm to David. David still keeps some cattle and grows barley, but Bridge Farm itself was demolished in 2000. A planning application to replace the farmhouse was approved and the footings for a new house put in, but approval has subsequently been rescinded by AVDC to the couple's disappointment and confusion.

Orchard Croft, where David and Val still live, is a brick-built house constructed by David himself. A chalet-style bungalow with dormer windows upstairs, the house has three bedrooms and one large public room. Their son and daughter were brought up here, attending school in Aston Clinton and then Aylesbury. Both are now grown-up and living in Aylesbury and Cambridge respectively.

As long-term residents, David and Val remember many former villagers. They clearly recall the Sanders family who owned Broadview Farm in the 1960s and William Moorhouse who bought Broadview Farm from the Sanders in 1971 and who changed it from a milking farm to a pig farm.

David and Val have talked occasionally about leaving the village, which they have always found a friendly and pleasant place to live, but think on the whole it is unlikely that they will do so unless circumstances make this necessary. They consider the village too small to sustain facilities like a shop, and would in any case be happy to see it remain much as it is at present.

THE OLD SCHOOL HOUSE

Edward, Helen & David Lonsdale

THE OLD RECTORY

Bob & Marion Woodman

ORCHARD CROFT

David & Valerie Lake

The Old School House

Built in 1844 by the Church of England (and largely as a result of the efforts of the then Rector, Reverend William Hastings Kelk) as a National School for up to 46 primary school-aged pupils, the Old School House occupies a corner plot on what were originally the glebe lands of St Mary's Church. The Old Rectory is close by as is the former Rectory Farm (also called Glebe or Church Farm). A plaque in a gable wall on the schoolhouse is inscribed "National School 1844". Kelly's Post Office Directories from 1847 onwards describe the building as a "neat and commodious schoolhouse" with a surprising capacity of sixty pupils. "The Era" newspaper of December 1844 records that the Queen Dowager (Adelaide, widow of William IV) sent a donation of £20 towards the expenses of building the new school and teacher's residence.

Constructed of old chequer brick and with a slate roof, this was a single-room school, with a small room at the rear serving as the schoolhouse to accommodate the schoolmistress and her family. There is evidence that at one time a staircase led – either inside or outside the building – to another small room above. As the Old School House is a grade II listed building there are major restrictions as to the kind of changes which can be made. At some stage, a kitchen and a bedroom above it were built behind the schoolhouse by local builder Stanley Ward, and a garage was erected at the side of the building by the couple from whom the current owners bought the house. The main entrance was originally situated centrally in the front wall of the building and although it has been sealed off its outline is still evident, whilst a bricked-up door at the rear of the schoolroom has in recent years been reopened. A false ceiling has at some point been constructed above the schoolroom. The old staircase has also gone although a section of the wooden banister is still visible, but now embedded in a wall. A new hall has replaced the old "lean-to" which seems to have served as a kitchen during the 1960s and 1970s. The house now consists of three bedrooms and a study in addition to the large room which was originally the schoolroom.

During the sixty years of its life as an infant school, Drayton Beauchamp School had only four schoolmistresses. The first, paid £5 per year, was Ann Stratford whose husband Robert was a gardener and also Clerk to the village church's Vestry Committee for 52 years. The couple had at least twelve children of their own born between 1848 and 1866 so the cramped nature of their living quarters can only be imagined. The "Church Book" kept by the churchwardens to record expenses talks about Robert Stratford being paid to dig wells and to weed in the churchyard while his wife was paid to clean the church and wash the surplices. In the 1881 Census Ann is listed as schoolmistress, Julia (one of Ann's daughters) is listed as nineteen years old and a teacher, and Julia's brother William, fifteen, is a "pupil teacher". In 1886 Julia Stratford married William Price, a butler who was born in Great Kimble and who in the 1881 Census is listed as a servant to the Jenney family at Drayton Lodge. (In 1913 William's brother Arthur married Nellie Ball, one of the seven children of Walter and Elizabeth Ball whose family features so largely in Drayton Beauchamp village life. As Walter Ball's mother was a Hedges by birth, the kinship interconnections between three large village families – Hedges, Ball and Stratford – begin to be evident).

In the Kelly's Directory of 1887 Julia Price is named as village schoolmistress with an average pupil attendance of ten. Presumably her mother Ann Stratford had retired by then. By the time of the 1891 Census, Julia and William Price had left the village with their two little boys, and Ann and Robert Stratford, both 69, were living in a cottage elsewhere in Drayton Beauchamp. Ann Stratford died in 1898 aged 76 and Robert in November 1901 aged 80, seven months after his name last appears on the census return. By 1891, the schoolmistress was Georgina Hayler (born in Kent), aged 25, who was sharing the schoolhouse with her mother Emily. Emily was said to be a retired schoolmistress aged 47 and born in Surrey. School attendance still averaged ten. Georgina and Emily Hayler do not appear in village census records either before or after 1891, but Georgina Hayler is still listed as the village schoolmistress in the Kelly's Directory of 1895, with an average attendance of nine infants.

The Kelly's Directory of 1899 names Marion Horwood as schoolmistress with an average school attendance of twelve. Marion was a daughter of John Horwood, farmer at Manor (Morgans) Farm, and was eighteen in 1899. By 1901 she is listed in the census as living with her family at Manor Farm and there is no mention in this census of the school or the schoolhouse. The school had permanently stopped functioning as a school by 1903, there being by then fewer than ten pupils on average. (Indeed a Church Parish Magazine of April 1881 talks of there being "no regular school" in the village even then and the Kelly's Directory of that year states that the school was being used "for parochial purposes"). The older children had for several years attended schools in other parishes, but by 1903 even the youngest children walked to school in Wilstone or Aston Clinton. In the 1911 Census the school was said to be "uninhabited" and Marion Horwood is once again listed at Manor Farm where she was helping her father with the work of the farm.

On 4th December 1894 the very first Drayton Beauchamp Parish Meeting was held in the schoolroom. This meeting was convened according to the 1894 Local Government Act which codified the principles so strongly held by the Liberals under Gladstone - i.e. that a democratic voting structure should replace the traditional power of the Tory Rector and Squire. Ironically, the local Lord of the Manor Stewart William Jenney of Drayton Manor (as Drayton Lodge was now called) was appointed Chairman at this first Meeting, to be replaced the following year by the Rector. Annual Parish Meetings continued to be held in the schoolroom for the next 67 years with all matters important to the village discussed. These included, for many years, the annual appointment of the Village Constables and the Overseers of the Poor. Reading back through the Minutes of these long-ago Meetings, it is clear that the same issues recur periodically over the years: the lack of street lighting, gas and mains drainage, the problem of vehicles speeding through the village, and similar issues which continue to be enthusiastically debated - even if not resolved - at 21st Century Parish Meetings where officialdom and formality do not silence local voices.

Between 1911 and 1960 the schoolhouse appears to have served as a home for many of the tenant farmers of Rectory Farm which was also owned by the Church of England. Presumably these tenants were restricted to the living quarters at the rear of the building because the Parish Meeting minutes of 1921 talk about a village Social Club being formed and the Rector allowing the old schoolroom to be used for its meetings. The room was also used as a Sunday School venue and for many village social events – for instance at the end of the Second World War when a party was held so that money collected locally for returning servicemen (of whom there were at least fourteen) could be distributed, and a belated tea at New Year, 1948, for the forty children of the parish to commemorate Victory Day. In 1953 villagers gathered there to watch the Coronation on a television which had been hired specially for the occasion. Several old photographs of village gatherings can be seen to have been taken in the schoolroom.

In 1947 the schoolroom was acknowledged to be in a dilapidated state and in need of repairs which would cost £40. Older villagers remember volunteering to help repair and decorate the room which was still being used as a social centre. By 1960 the Church had decided that the Rectory, Rectory Farm and the whole school building were all surplus to requirements and should be sold. In that year, a meeting of the Parochial Church Council held in the schoolroom discussed the future of the building and concluded that they could not afford the purchase price (£600) required by the Diocesan Education Committee for the schoolroom, schoolhouse and garden. They, along with the Rectory and Rectory Farm, were therefore sold privately by the Church of England to Michael and Ann Adams. The final annual Parish Meeting was held in the schoolroom on 29th March 1961 and chaired by Sir John Guillum Scott, who was by then living at Lower Farm. Thereafter, the Old School House became the home of housekeepers employed at the Old Rectory until 1979 when it was sold as a separate dwelling. On 3rd December 1994 a special Parish Meeting was held in the Old School House to celebrate the centenary of the very first Parish Meeting, with villagers attending appropriately dressed in the styles of 1894.

David and Helen Lonsdale

In 1990 David and Helen Lonsdale, the current owners, bought the property. David and Helen met whilst working in London and married in 1969. David comes from Clapham while Helen was brought up in Barnet. Helen's family, interestingly, farmed many years ago in the nearby village of Lilley in the Luton area and she is related to the famous Charles Irons, Luton's town crier for many years until his death in 1940. David and Helen lived previously in East Barnet and whilst Helen was raising their family, David was a Sales Director of printing companies in

London. In 1991 they moved to the Old School House and David subsequently secured a position in 1994 as London Sales Director with Maund & Irvine Ltd, the printing firm in Tring. He retired in 2006. Their son Edward, then a teenager, moved to Drayton Beauchamp with them. Sadly, their daughter Elizabeth died in October 1990.

David and Helen love the village and feel happily established as part of the community. They themselves are acknowledged to be particularly good at organising walks, expeditions and charity events which bring villagers together, thereby fostering the happy memories and community spirit so vital in a small village.

Party at School House 1949

Christmas Party in the School House 1947/1948

Frank Smith helping wounded comrade after Dunkirk evacuation 1940

The Old Rectory

The oldest known document pertaining to the Drayton Beauchamp Rectory is a mortgage deed dated 29th May 1828. It is known that an older Rectory had stood on the same glebe lands - a fact confirmed by an etching in the church and in the 1607 Glebe Terriers survey which talks too about a village green standing in the same area. The exact position of the original Rectory is, however, not known and no legal deeds were drawn up because there was no transfer of ownership since the building stood on Church land. In Volume 3 of the "History and Antiquities of the County of Buckinghamshire", 1847, George Lipscomb M.D. writes that a Rectory existed in Drayton Beauchamp in 1291, but was pulled down in 1826 and a new one built. (In fact, a section of the County Council's website "Unlocking Buckinghamshire's Past" asserts that the Rectory does indeed sit on the same site as the Rectory occupied by Richard Hooker in 1584.) In the cellars of the current building are the remains of very old foundations which could mark the position of the original Rectory.

In 1828 the parish of Drayton Beauchamp still came under the Lincoln Diocese, and in that year a counterpart mortgage of £538 3s 8d was given by Queen Anne's Bounty (a fund established in 1704 to provide financial assistance for poorer clergy) to Basil Woodd, the resident Rector of the time who was also a hymn-writer, the author of many publications, and a founder of several schools. The current building, Grade II listed, is believed to date from 1826/8 and was originally a square, typically Georgian brick-built house with a chimney at each side of the slate roof. It is likely that it was built privately but there are no papers naming the architect or documenting the building of the house. In 1895 a bathroom, kitchen and scullery were added. In 1927 electricity was installed along with a motor for pumping water from two of the several wells. In 1932 a garage and approach road from the Holloway were built. In 1937 the house acquired mains water.

By 1937, the Reverend Henry Burkitt, long-time Rector, had been replaced by the Reverend Charles Bayliss with his wife Agnes and son Lloyd who lived in the Rectory until 1939 when the Reverend William Augustus Wilson became Rector for a short time. In 1940 the Reverend D J Scurry Jones took up residence in the Aston Clinton Rectory. That same year, the Drayton Beauchamp Rectory was requisitioned, initially for evacuees, and then until October 1947 as a hostel for women from the Women's Land Army. A new bathroom was built for its young residents, the kitchen range was removed, and a new range large enough to cook for twenty girls was installed.

The Electoral Registers for 1945-8 list a succession of women living there. By coincidence, one of these young women was Doris Kempster, daughter of James and Annie who had lived at the thatched Cottage at the lower end of the village in the 1930s but had moved to Bucklandwharf in 1938. Doris's younger sister Betty recalls Doris describing how she would return fearfully to her new accommodation along the canal towpath and past the churchyard in the evenings after visiting her family.

The Old Rectory does not seem to have been used as a Rectory after 1940, and in November 1947 was rented to Guy and Ann Guillum Scott. Exactly three years later it was rented to their son John who, with his wife Elizabeth, lived there until 1960 when they purchased and moved to Lower Farm at the other end of the village. Guy Guillum Scott was Chancellor of Oxford Diocese and his son, Sir John, is described in his Oxford Biography entry as an ecclesiastical civil servant.

The Benefices of Drayton Beauchamp, Aston Clinton and Buckland were combined in 1963 but before that - in 1960 - the Old Rectory, Rectory Farm, the Schoolhouse and 24 acres of land were sold by the Diocese to Michael and Anne Adams who remained there until 1983. In 1962, Peggy Elvy is listed as "living in" just for one year at the Rectory where she was employed. The Adams made various changes to the layout of the house – for instance replacing the four original fireplaces and chimneys with a central fireplace, and adding a conservatory on the west side of the house. The Church has retained ownership of a narrow lane which leads through the Rectory fields to the church itself. The Adams at first used the schoolhouse to accommodate their housekeeper but in 1979 sold the schoolhouse and the schoolroom which was part of it.

The Old Rectory sits in around an acre and a half of garden surrounded by what used to be the glebe. Close to the Old Rectory and within the glebe stood Rectory Farm which, traditionally, was farmed by the resident Rector or Curate himself or by the residents of the schoolhouse. In a letter dated 1956, John Guillum Scott talks about recent tenants of the schoolhouse – a couple who had lived there for over twenty years (probably Alfred and Kathleen Knight who had moved there from Painesend Farm). They were followed by Cyril and Marjorie Spittles whose son John was Mick Anns' boyhood friend along with Pete Knight. Pete lived with the Spittles and worked with the horses at Lower Farm. The final tenant farmer was James Pemberton who left the village in 1959.

The original buildings at Rectory Farm comprised stables and a coaching yard, but these were then converted for cows, with a milking parlour - complete with unusual Victorian sliding windows- and pigsties in the yard. The cold cellars beneath the Old Rectory still have a shelved area on which milk churns would have been stored and the outline of a door leading directly from outside into the cellar is still visible. Water from the well in the yard would have been used to cool the milk. At least six cows were kept at one stage, and a milk round was organised from Rectory Farm.

The rich history of the area is illustrated by the discovery in 1993 in the Old

Rectory fields between the church and the Moat House of a decorated ring - quatrefoil petals holding an unpolished diamond (believed to be a well-used writing diamond) - dating from the 1500s. At a Coroner's Court in 1998 this ring was declared Treasure. As a substantial manor house, pulled down in 1760, stood on the site of what is now the Moat House and as a footpath led from the manor house to the Church, it is hardly surprising that a treasure such as this should be found, probably dropped by a person of some wealth walking between the two buildings. It is believed that there were cottages in the vicinity of the manor house, and their occupants too would have used the footpath which must originally have led to the Church but which now ends abruptly at a barbed wire fence. A silver cloak buckle with a bell inside and coins – Roman and of later date – have also been discovered in this area.

A further point of historical interest is the continuing cultivation at the Old Rectory of the "Cheiranthus Harpur-Crewe" – a miniature double-leafed yellow wallflower developed by the botanist and horticulturist Henry Harpur-Crewe (nephew of the 8th Baronet Sir George Crewe of Calke) while he was Rector of Drayton Beauchamp from 1860 until his death in 1883. A pink snowdrop he developed has, sadly, died out.   Trees planted around the Old Rectory date from the same era and are believed to have been planted by Henry too. Henry, described as a "charming and genial man", was a staunch Conservative and a "vigorous newspaper correspondent". He was also a member of the Council of the Royal Horticultural Society and particularly loved crocuses, snowdrops and tulips.   The Ipswich Journal of 25th September 1883 records that although many floral tributes were sent to his funeral by the rich and famous, "the only flowers placed on his grave were a wreath and cross made by his sisters from his favourite flowers in his own garden".

Bob and Marion Woodman

Bob and Christine Woodman bought the Old Rectory from Michael and Anne Adams in October 1983 and moved in some eight months later. They had been living in Tring but had been searching for a house in a rural setting. At that stage, Bob was working as a company director in London and the couple had one daughter at University and one still at school. Christine died in 1993. In 1996 Bob married Marion, a specialist nurse who also has two daughters, and brought her to live at the Old Rectory. (Bob originates from West Bromwich and Marion from Hull.) The two are happy in their lovely house with its excellent position and superb views, although they feel somewhat isolated geographically from the remainder of the village.   They echo the points put forward by many other residents – the lack of a social meeting place apart from the church and the tendency for people to drive through the village rather than walk.

Bob and Marion have worked hard to try to achieve a balance between modernising the house and restoring it in a way that is sympathetic to its original elegant appearance and character. They have no plans for further changes and do not intend to move away so long as they remain fit enough to look after the sheep which they see as an integral part of their estate and essential for keeping the grass under control.

St Mary the Virgin Church

St Mary's Church, a Grade I listed building, was founded either by William Count of Mortain or by his father Robert. Robert had accompanied his half-brother William the Conqueror from Normandy in 1066 and in recognition of his loyal service was awarded the land which later became the village of Drayton Beauchamp along with many other vast tracts of land in England (including Berkhamsted where he was instructed to build a castle).

The first mention of the church is at the beginning of the 13th century when the Manor of Drayton (Draitone) and patronage of the Rectory were held by William de Beauchamp, and it would seem that the name of the village is derived from him. As mentioned in the Introduction to this book, the lands then passed to the Cobham family who gave them to Edward III. Edward in turn gave them to his shield bearer, Thomas Cheney (or Cheyney or Cheyne) in 1364.

The Manor remained in the possession of the Cheyne family for almost four centuries and the moat of a Cheyne residence near the church remains. A marble monument in the chancel celebrates the life of William, Lord Cheyne, Viscount Newhaven, the last of his line. He died in 1728 aged 71 and after 48 years of marriage to Gertrude, Lady Cheyne, who was sister to Evelyn Pierrepoint, Duke of Kingston. Lady Cheyne began the monument which depicts her late husband but died before it was completed. Her kinswoman Mrs Gertrude Tolhurst completed the work, adding a second figure to represent Lady Cheyne. The inscription informs us that Mrs Tolhurst was so distressed by Lady Cheyne's death on 11th June 1732 that she committed suicide five weeks later.

It seems certain that there is a Cheyne vault beneath the chancel. A brass on the chancel floor apparently marks the grave of William Cheyne who died in 1375. Rev. Hastings Kelk in his 1854 "History of Drayton Beauchamp" tells us that the skeleton of Sir John Cheyne who died in 1468 aged almost 100, nearly seven feet tall and with a full set of teeth, was discovered when the floor of the chancel was dug up several centuries later. Sir John's first wife Joan, who died in 1445, and their newborn son Alexander, were buried beside him. Aged eighty, Sir John remarried - this time to Agnes, daughter of Sir William de Cogenhoe. This led to his becoming possessed of the manor and advowson of Cogenhoe as well as of Drayton Beauchamp.

Sir Francis Cheyne is recorded as having been buried in the church in 1619 and his wife Mary ten years later. In his Will, Francis states that he wants to be buried in the chancel of the village church, "as so many of my ancestors are".

An account of what happened to the Lordship of the Manor of Drayton Beauchamp and the patronage of the village church after 1728 can be found in the chapter about Drayton Manor. After Stewart William Jenney, the last Lord of the Manor to live locally, died in 1948, unmarried and without heirs, the lordship was taken over by his uncle's descendants in Norfolk. In 1999, the last member of the family, Airmyne Harpur-Crewe, who had been born a Jenney but who took, as her brothers had done, the surname Harpur-Crewe when she became the heiress of Sir Vauncey Harpur-Crewe, died without heir. The patrons of the church since then are the Bishop of Oxford and Mr A Roger Pegg of Ticknall, Derbyshire. Mr Pegg, co-executor of Airmyne Harpur-Crewe's Will, sits on the selection board when a new Rector is to be appointed and is kept informed of major events which are to take place in the church so that he can attend if he wishes.

The present church dates from the fifteenth century when it was restored and partly reconstructed using some of the materials from the earlier church which, it is believed, was constructed in the early thirteenth century. The Norman font dates from the twelfth century. The Apostles Window at the East end and several other stained glass windows date back to the fifteenth century and others were installed in the early nineteenth century in memory of members of the Griffin family. The church has a nave with two aisles and a chancel, and a square tower at the west end. A porch was added in 1500.

The Hull Packet and East Riding Times of 25th August 1854 records the escape from Tring Lock-Up of "a determined fellow" who had been "incarcerated, after a desperate conflict, he being charged with stealing two hundredweight of lead from the church". The man had, however, escaped from the lock-up and was believed to have fled to London. The theft of lead from churches is, sadly, not a recent phenomenon. During the ten years after this theft it was recognised that substantial work was required to repair St Mary's. Over the course of two years the church was restored at considerable cost, and a pulpit built to commemorate the great Anglican theologian Richard Hooker, incumbent from 1584-5. The Reverend Henry Harpur-Crewe, rector from 1860-83 and a distinguished naturalist and horticulturist, officiated at the re-opening service in January 1867. The Archdeacon read a lesson, the Bishop of Oxford preached the sermon, and a hymn composed for the occasion was sung. Between that service and the evening one, the sum of £133 was raised for the Church Restoration Fund.

An oak reredos was placed in the chancel in 1887 in memory of the Reverend Harpur-Crewe. There are three bells inscribed 1621, 1704 and 1773. Church baptismal records go back to 1538, burial records to 1653 and marriage records to 1541.

A mural tablet records the deaths of two village men killed during the Great War – Ernest Thomas Kempster, AB, who went down with the Queen Mary at the Battle of Jutland on 31st May 1916 aged nineteen and Lance Corporal Frank John ("Jack") Hedges of the 76th Battalion Canadian Regiment who is listed as having been killed during the capture of Vimy Ridge on 14th April 1917 aged 25 (although the Canadian Expeditionary Force Burial Register in fact records the date of his death – "killed in action" - as 5th April 1917). A third local man, Francis John Smith of Hang Hill, a Gunner in the Royal Artillery, who died on 28th March 1945 aged 36, is honoured on the Tring War Memorial and buried in Tring Cemetery.

In the 19th century St Mary's Church had two exceptionally long-serving Clerks to the Vestry Committee. Thomas Kipping who died in 1845 had been Clerk for 47 years. Four years later, Robert Stratford – husband of the schoolmistress – took Thomas's place and remained Clerk for 52 years until he died in 1901. In 1922 the church's Vestry Meetings became the Church Parochial Council, and women's names begin to appear in the minutes.

Included in a list of Vicars of the church are Ralph, installed in 1220 and Peter de Draitone, installed in 1233. Among the Rectors listed are Miles de Beauchamp (1269-79), Richard de Draitone (1279-1307), Richard Hooker (1584-85), Robert Cheyne (1662-89) and William Hastings Kelk the historian (1840-60). (Two letters dated 1848 which survive among the correspondence of Samuel Wilberforce, bishop of Oxford and third son of the famous William Wilberforce) address a disagreement which had arisen between Kelk and William Christopher/Jenney and entreat each man to make his peace with the other.)

The "Reports of the Commissioners" of 1815-35 identify those such as the Lord of the Manor and other wealthy local farmers who paid towards the relief of the poor in the parish, money which would be distributed in the church. The 1838 Tithe Map identifies the individual farmers who were renting the extensive areas of glebe land. The Rector of the time, the Reverend Thomas Naylor Bland, owned the parsonage house, a cottage, yard, barns and fields – a total of two acres three furlongs and 38 perches. The 1836 Tithe Commutation Act had changed the old system whereby tithes were paid to the church in the form of produce. This had resulted in a loss of incentive to make improvements to one's fields in that the more crops were grown, the more produce had to be given to the local church. Now, money payment based on the size of tithable areas of land was brought in, hence the careful detail of the Tithe Map and accompanying Apportionment Document. Each building, field and crop in the parish is itemised, the size of every individual area is calculated, and the owner and the occupier of each painstakingly noted.

The Compton Census of 1676 reported 83 conformists and twelve non-conformists resident in the parish, while an Ecclesiastical Census of 30th March 1851 recorded seventy people in both the morning and afternoon congregation. An 1848 book entitled 'A Topographical Dictionary of England' edited by Samuel Lewis states that "the Rectory of Drayton Beauchamp is valued in the King's books at £11 9s 7d and in the patronage of William Jenney Esq.". It adds that "tithes have been commuted for £304-15s 0d and the glebe comprises 28 acres."

The "Drayton Church Book" kept by the churchwardens and covering the years from 1829 until 1918 provides a fascinating insight into the physical labours which went on in and around the church. There are lists of organists and sextons, of those who cleaned the church and washed the surplices, and of those who weeded the churchyard – including the wonderfully named Shadrack Dunton in 1835 - and dug drains and "dead wells". (These seem to have been some form of soakaway dug to receive excess water which would then gradually dissipate into the surrounding area. Perhaps the leaking canal caused particular problems in the land around the church.) Baby sparrows were bought and flies were swept. The organ was pumped by boys and men whose names - Kempster, Ball and Hedges - are still familiar in the village.

Mention is made in numerous books and papers of the unusual practice in Drayton Beauchamp of "Stephening". This took place on 26th December, St Stephen's Day, when the entire village would visit the Rectory to enjoy, at the Rector's expense, as much bread, cheese and ale as they wanted. It seems that John Lockman, Rector from 1746-1808, decided to discontinue the practice which he believed led to drunkenness and greed. On the appropriate day he hid with his housekeeper in the Rectory while furious villagers beat on the doors trying to gain entry and loudly accusing him of being parsimonious. Eventually the villagers stormed the Rectory and ate and drank whatever they could find there. Stephening was thus re-introduced against the helpless Rector's wishes until his successor, Basil Woodd, who in 1808 was presented to the living by the Right Honourable Mary Manners, the Lord of the Manor, decided instead to give an annual sum of money in proportion to the number of villagers. When, however, the population of the village rose sharply, Basil Woodd began to question the need to continue with this payment, and stopped it around 1827, four years before he died. In 1834 the Charities Commission investigated the matter, taking evidence from some of the irate villagers, but they found that there was nothing laid down in law to force the Rector to give either money or ale and food to the villagers, and no trace either of the origin or the meaning of the custom, which accordingly ended for ever.

In 1940 the Benefice became a plurality with Aston Clinton and the new Rector, the Reverend D J Scurry Jones, took up residence in the Aston Clinton Rectory. The parishes of Drayton Beauchamp and Aston Clinton were combined into a Benefice with Buckland on 14th November, 1963. The Rectory, Rectory Farm and farm buildings, schoolhouse and 24 acres of land had already been sold by the Diocese in 1960 to a private buyer. The schoolhouse was used as a centre for village meetings and social events for many years until it was sold as a private house, but for the past fifty years St Mary the Virgin Church has been the only public building in the parish.

MORGANS FARM May 1973

ST MARY THE VIRGIN CHURCH, DRAYTON BEAUCHAMP

The Moat House

The Moat House is situated in one of the most historically important areas of the parish of Drayton Beauchamp. It is close to the church whose origins can be traced back to the twelfth century and close also to the site of the original Rectory. Around The Moat House are a series of homestead moats and fishponds which, in England, tend to date from between the mid twelfth and early fourteenth centuries although the oldest moats in Buckinghamshire are probably Saxon according to the Victoria County History. Artificially created by the digging of ditches, moats were intended to demonstrate the high status of the owner as well as having a secondary defensive role against the attacks of both humans and animals. Pevsner and Williamson in their book "The Buildings of England – Buckinghamshire" assert that where moats are adjacent to fishponds (as in Drayton Beauchamp) this emphasises their manorial character.

In addition to its close proximity to the church, The Moat House stands on land where formerly stood the original Cheyne manor house, which would have been approached along an avenue bordered by rows of trees northwest of the church. No trace of this building now remains although some "unfrogged bricks, carved stone window mullions and a wooden pile" (according to the 'Unlocking Buckinghamshire's Past' website) were discovered in that area some years ago. A magnificent manor house is, however, clearly depicted on the 1736 "Mapp of the Mannour of Drayton Beauchamp". This mansion was built, it is believed, in the 15th century by the Cheney/Cheyne/Cheyney family, Lords of the Manor of Drayton Beauchamp from 1364. As the Cheynes were also Lords of the Manor of Chesham Bois, it is not completely clear which manor house was home to which generation of the family. Drayton Beauchamp Burial Registers record, however, that several Cheynes lie buried in the chancel of the village church, as is more fully described in the chapter on St Mary the Virgin Church.

Francis Cheyne wrote in his Will of 1619 that he wished to be buried in the village church beside his ancestors and that he wanted his wife to remain after his death in Drayton Beauchamp in the house where they had lived for so long together. It seems likely, however, that his nephew and heir, also called Francis, built the Dower House among the main group of village cottages for his widowed aunt and kept the manor house for his own use. After the last Cheyne Lord of the Manor died and the Gumleys built a new manor house for themselves as described in the chapter on Drayton Manor, the original manor house near the church fell into disrepair and was pulled down in 1760. Villagers of old used to talk of a ghostly milkmaid who ran between Upper Farm and an ancient cottage beside the moats, but whether she "belonged to" the era of the original manor house or not is unknown.

A new cottage had been built in this area by 1838 when the Tithe Map and Apportionment Document were drawn up, listing William Christopher/Jenney as the owner of a house, meadow, water and eleven acres of land, and Fanny Brown as the occupier. In the 1841 Census, Benjamin Brown, farmer aged sixty, Fanny Brown aged 55 and Charlotte Brown aged seventy, are listed in the village enumeration but – as is so often the case in Drayton Beauchamp - without an address. In the Buckinghamshire Posse Comitatus of 1798 Benjamin, John and Joseph Brown are listed as farmers. John Brown is said to keep seven horses, two wagons and three carts, but he and Joseph may have belonged to the Brown family who lived beyond Oakengrove at the southern tip of the parish in an area which at that time still came within the parish boundaries of Drayton Beauchamp. From 1879, each successive tenant of Upper Farm – Richard Horwood senior followed by Richard Horwood junior, and then in 1913 by Harry Dwight - rented from the Jenney estate the Moat House, water and eleven acres of land, sub-letting Moat Cottage itself (as it was then being called) and a few acres. Harry Dwight bought Upper Farm, Moat Cottage and the surrounding land in or around 1914.

In the 1851 Census, John Howlett (48), a gardener, and his wife Ann (51) were living at Moat Cottage with their son Thomas (20), an agricultural labourer. From 1851 until at least 1939, the Howlett family continued to be tenants of this house. Thomas and Ann had seven children or more, two of whom, both named William, died in early childhood in the 1870s. Thomas's grandson Harry, born in 1879, is listed in the Drayton Church Book as being Sexton in the village church for several years from 1896.

The final occupants of Moat Cottage were John Howlett's son, also John (born 1859), an agricultural labourer at Morgan's Farm, and the younger John's sister Elizabeth (born in 1865). Neither ever married. In the Census of 1881 the younger John is listed at an Aylesbury address, working as groom for a magistrate whose late wife was, I believe, Eliza Rodwell, eldest child of Thomas and Ann Rodwell of Lower Farm, Drayton Beauchamp. On 1st November 1890 John enlisted for twelve years in the East Surrey Regiment of Infantry, but he appears from the records to have been very unhappy in the Army from the start and had returned surreptitiously to Moat Cottage within four months, never to leave home again. The Army valued at £2 11s 6½d the kit he had taken with him when he deserted, but whether this cost was ever recovered is not recorded. John died in 1935 aged 75 and Elizabeth (Lizzie) in 1947 aged 82 at 100 Bierton Hill, Aylesbury, the former Poor Law Union Workhouse. (This was built in 1844, changed its name after 1904 to "100 Bierton Road" and during the Second World War became a general hospital known as Tindal Hospital.) Both John and Lizzie are buried in the village churchyard. People who lived in the village in the 1930s and 40s still remember Lizzie Howlett and the practical acts of kindness of the village women towards the old lady.

John and Eleanor Tonkinson

Lizzie's "shanty" was pulled down around 1950 and at some stage a second cottage which had stood in the area of the moats was also demolished. A new Moat House was built, probably by J. Chandler and Son, the land having been sold by Harry Nicholls, by this time owner of Upper Farm, to John and Eleanor Tonkinson. An engraved beam over the door lintel gives the date of finishing the work as being 1951. John, an RAF doctor, spent his working life being posted to various parts of the world. Twin daughters Jennifer Anne (Jenny) and Gillian Sally (Sally) were born in South Africa in 1941 where Dr Tonkinson was Commanding Officer of a medical establishment for the treatment of pilots undergoing training for the War. The family returned to England on a troopship in 1945. Stationed then at RAF Halton and living in Wendover, Dr and Mrs Tonkinson were keen to find what they hoped would become a permanent family home in England and were delighted when they found the ideal location in Drayton Beauchamp in which to build this home.

The new Moat House was a white brick house in the shape of a "T" with a green slate roof and green metal window frames. The house consisted of a kitchen, bathroom, one large public room and two bedrooms on the ground floor with a third bedroom upstairs. The family later added a garage (which replaced an old Nissan hut used as a garage) and built a large room above it. The house stood in 3½ acres of land with a moat running around the circumference, apart from a marshy area to the right of the bridge which crosses the moat and leads to the property.

The family loved Drayton Beauchamp and their home there, and stayed longer in this house than in any other during the girls' childhood. The girls went to boarding school in Bedford from the age of seven or eight but spent happy holidays in the village with their ponies, cats, dogs, geese and chickens. They remember vividly the winter of 1952/3 when snow lay so deeply that "walking along the lane" meant walking above the tops of the hedgerow. (In November 1952 the snowdrifts in Whipsnade village, only a few miles away, were measured and discovered to be eight feet high.) The girls also recalled parties held in the Schoolhouse for the visually impaired children who had been evacuated to Drayton Manor. The girls' mother Eleanor Tonkinson was an avid gardener who designed a wonderful garden with long herbaceous borders, large lawns on two levels, a rose garden and a kitchen garden. Eleanor enjoyed her work as a councillor serving on the Planning Committee of Aylesbury Rural District Council and was involved in 1955 when the two Morgans Cottages were bought, demolished, and rebuilt by the Council as 1 and 2 Beauchamp Cottages. The girls' maternal grandmother, Diana Bird, travelled with the family to their many postings, and lived for several years in a caravan in the gardens of The Moat House.

Sadly, the family's wish to remain in Drayton Beauchamp came to an end when Dr

Tonkinson, by now a Group Captain, was posted first to Germany in 1957 and then to Aden in 1962. The family bought a house in Watford and Jenny believes that her parents rented out the Moat House for a few years to the Gibson family before reluctantly deciding that they should sell it. This they did in 1962 to William and Sheila Moorhouse. John Tonkinson died in 1993 and Eleanor in 1996. Their daughters now live at a distance from Drayton Beauchamp, but Jenny has returned several times to revisit the village and her much-loved childhood home.

William and Sheila Moorhouse

In 1962 William and Sheila Moorhouse moved to the Moat House from Aylesbury. Bill Moorhouse was a member of the well-known Moorhouse family whose "William Moorhouse and Sons" jam-making business was established in 1887 in Leeds. The business expanded to Aylesbury in 1956 with the building of the Sunglow Model Factory on the Bierton Road. Three years later the firm was bought by Schweppes and in 1969 it merged with Cadbury's.

At the time of their move, the Moorhouses had two sons, Colin aged seven and John, six, and a daughter, Karen, four. A younger sister Amanda was born at the Moat House soon afterwards. Sheila Moorhouse, another talented gardener, carried out an enthusiastic landscaping project at Moat House, creating an orchard, flower meadow and borders alongside a vast vegetable plot. She won numerous prizes for her garden produce and cut flowers at the local horticultural shows. Jim Anns, who had worked at the Moorhouse jam factory, now became gardener at The Moat House, helping with the upkeep of the extensive gardens.

The Moat House in 1962 was a dormer bungalow which the Moorhouses enlarged upwards at the back, creating more bedroom space. The large lounge downstairs was ideal for parties, while the gardens, moats and surrounding countryside offered unlimited potential for children to explore and enjoy.

Karen Brown (née Moorhouse) remembers an idyllic childhood in Drayton Beauchamp. She recalls sledging in the field near her home in the winter of 1962/3, with a wet finish to the run if the sledge did not stop before tumbling into the moat. The outfit she wore to attend a celebratory fête held in the Old Rectory gardens around 1970 is still clear in her mind's eye, as are the village residents of the time who were such an important part of her childhood – particularly Gordon and Margaret Nicholls at Upper Farm.

The Moorhouse children attended primary school in Aylesbury, and although a school bus collected secondary school children at the crossroads with the B489, at all other times public transport was available only by walking to Aston Clinton or up the Holloway to the Crow's Nest. Karen recalls walking to the Rothschild Arms

Pub at Buckland to wait for the school bus on wet days as the pub had an outdoor toilet which could be used for shelter, the children taking it in turn to look out for the approaching bus.

In 1971 Bill and Sheila had Broadview House built. They then moved there, selling The Moat House to the current owners.

The Bungalow, 1 Church Lane

This four-bedroomed bungalow constructed of special handmade bricks was built in 1974 by Stanley Ward on land sold to him by Gordon Nicholls of Upper Farm. As the address suggests, the house sits on the narrow lane leading to the field in which St Mary's Church is sited. The Old Schoolhouse faces it across the lane, the Old Rectory is between the Schoolhouse and the church, and the Moat House is set back at the far end of the lane.

Stanley Ward, a stonemason who worked on several Oxford University buildings, met Evelyn in 1948 while he was home on leave during his two years of National Service, and the two married four years later. Both originated from Oxfordshire, but moved to Buckinghamshire when Stanley went into partnership with his brother, an electrician, as a house builder. He and Evelyn were living in Buckland immediately before moving to Drayton Beauchamp with their son and daughter. Both children attended secondary school in Aylesbury and often walked across the fields or along the canal towards Tring Hill to catch the bus to school. Stanley died suddenly in 1989 and is buried in the village churchyard, close to the home in which Evelyn still lives.

John and Evelyn Seaton

In 1991 Evelyn remarried, her husband John Seaton having been widowed at almost exactly the same time as she herself had been. John was born in Stone, Buckinghamshire but lived for many years in Scotland. His training as a chef and Evelyn's as a bookkeeper have proved invaluable in recent years as the catering business they have established has become ever busier. John's other major interest is his garden, and the couple have for several years organised an annual plant sale to raise funds for charity – a popular event which draws people from far afield.

Evelyn was a Churchwarden at St Mary the Virgin Church for over twenty years and she, along with Peggy Elvy, spent many happy hours cleaning the church both inside and out. John, meantime, cut the grass in the churchyard for over ten years. Evelyn was also Lay Chairman of Wendover Deanery Synod for six years and a member of the Oxford Diocesan Synod serving on the boards of the Buildings Committee and the Patronage Board. Her church work meant frequent travel to Diocesan House, Oxford and to other churches and rectories over a wide area.

Placed as they are at right angles to, and slightly apart from, the main village lane, John and Evelyn see few villagers although many ramblers pass the house. They believe that most residents have moved to Drayton Beauchamp in search of privacy and quietness, hence the lack of social occasions involving the village in general. The absence of a "village centre" or of a public building apart from the church exacerbates this problem.

Evelyn and John have no plans for changes to their home, but acknowledge that at some point in the future it might be difficult for them to manage their large bungalow and garden.

THE BUNGALOW, CHURCH LANE

John & Evelyn Seaton

BADGERS END

Brooke & Warr-King Families

TREASURES

Graham & Terry Everson

Badgers End

Now a substantial family home set in five acres of land, Badgers End – so-named by Rosemary Brooke, the current owner - was originally made up of two tiny one-bedroomed cottages known as 3 and 4 Lower Farm Cottages, Rose Cottages, or Ballad Cottages. (The other two cottages belonging to Lower Farm were those now combined to form the one house now called Setherwood.)

Michael Anns of 2 Peartree Cottages recalls that when he was a child in the late 1940s, Joseph and Margaret Gomm lived in one of the cottages which now constitute Badgers End, and that his mother Margery used to work as housekeeper there. An aunt and uncle of his, Clara and Arthur Ball, also lived in one of the cottages for some time. Rosalie Hicks, Mary Stillwell and Caroline and Harry Rainbow lived there in the 1950s, Harry being a farm worker at Lower Farm. Earlier, when Mick's mother (born in 1916) was a child, residents of one of the cottages ran a village shop from their front room. There were several wells and a pump in the garden.

Rosemary Brooke and Moira Warr-King

In May 1959 Rosemary and Peter Brooke bought the two Rose Cottages, by then very dilapidated, from Florrie and Edie Ballad shortly before the two sisters moved to The Homestead, later named Setherwood. The Brookes could not move in for several months until essential work had been carried out to combine the cottages and make them habitable. Both Rosemary and Peter worked for Wellcome Cooper in Berkhamsted and had been searching for a rural property within easy commuting distance. They moved from Little Gaddesden to Drayton Beauchamp with their first child, then barely one year old; a second son and a daughter were born after they moved. They had to carry out considerable upgrading and renovation, employing Honours of Tring but doing much of the work themselves. A driveway had to be laid, one of the two staircases had to be removed, a garage added, and later a "granny annexe" built for Rosemary's parents who came from Yorkshire to live with them two years after they themselves moved in. The final changes were to extend the kitchen and to build a conservatory. The attic was converted after the heavy snowfalls of 1962 resulted in snow blowing under the roof tiles so that the roof had to be retiled, snow damage being a common problem locally that winter. Rosemary and Peter, although both ill at the time, were obliged to shovel large amounts of snow out through the window at the end of the attic and down into the garden.

During the digging for the foundations of the garage they discovered a penny dated 1745, and believe that this could have been put there to mark the year in which the cottages were built. Further evidence is the type of flinty brick used in the construction of the walls of the original cottages. The original floors were tiled with small floor tiles which were recycled to use as a path in front of the house, but wooden weatherboarding was used on the walls of the granny annexe as the original bricks could not be matched. There is a very old fireplace in what would have been the main room of one of the cottages, and a fireplace and the site of a brick oven in the other.

Rosemary felt welcomed to the village from the start and has many happy memories of her fifty years as a resident of Drayton Beauchamp. Parish Meetings when she and Peter moved here were held in the schoolhouse, with the church used as the other village meeting place. Rosemary has always played a full part in village life and activities and Peter was for many years Chairman of the Parish Meeting.

Maureen and Michael Hannon who lived in one of the "Upper Farm Cottages" opposite (now combined into one property called Genista) had a child of the same age as their older son, and the two families became friends. Their little boy played too with twins Alan and Arthur Kempster who lived at Sunnyside on the opposite side of the lane, and with Elizabeth and Catherine Anns, Mick's daughters. Rosemary and Peter were friends with Kevin and Patricia Fitzpatrick at Church Hill Farm, with John and Eleanor Tonkinson at The Moat House, and with Alfred Reynolds and his sister Edith at the Dower House where memorable parties were held.

In winter they skated on the original pond between Beauchamp Barn and Setherwood. Peter Brooke and Stanley Ward formed a fishing syndicate, renting the medieval moats at The Moat House from John Tonkinson's successors William and Sheila Moorhouse and stocking them with trout. On at least one occasion poachers were apprehended by the two men. The Brookes made hay in their field and were helped with the building of stooks or coils by Edie and Florrie Ballad, experienced countrywomen. The field at different times was used for horses, goats, geese, ducks, pheasants, lambs and ewes – the latter leading to memorable days dipping sheep with Derrick Ball of Broadview House. The garden was gradually extended into the field, and in 1961 a beech hedge was planted to mark the end of the garden. This hedge had to be replanted when hares ate it in its entirety. Later, a stable and a somewhat uneven grass tennis court were added.

Once Rosemary's parents came to live with them, and thanks to the elderly couple's sociability and interest in other people, Rosemary and Peter began to meet many of the older villagers too. Rosemary's father walked to Tring nearly every day, even in his 90s, and became close friends with Harry Nicholls of Upper Farm, particularly after the two men realised that they had both fought at Gallipoli. (Rosemary has recently discovered her father's memoirs in the attic, meticulously kept journals for 1915-1917.) Her mother, meanwhile, would preside over "proper tea parties", sometimes entertaining Anne Adams from the

Rectory and Lady Elizabeth Scott from Lower Farm. Rosemary's mother died in August 1972 and her father a few months later. Her brother-in-law died suddenly in the same period, so Badgers End became – and has remained – a real family home with Rosemary's sister, brother, niece, children and now grandchildren and other members of the extended family all welcomed and accommodated very frequently. Her sister Moira Warr-King came to live there in 1973 after being widowed, and Moira's husband Tony is buried in the village churchyard. Peter Brooke died in 1992.

Rosemary continues to live happily in the village, maintaining her interests in the church (where she is a Churchwarden) and in sport, music, Bridge, Italian and animals. She feels that the village remains a friendly community with a strong informal support system, but recognises that some people move to a village such as this because they seek quietness and do not want to join in local activities. Life in general seems busier too, and more people drive rather than walk. Perhaps, she believes, more effort could be made to include new residents in village life, with friendly introductions offered at an early stage, but these overtures need to have a positive response if they are to succeed. She hopes the village will not develop too much more for fear that it will lose its rural charm and attractiveness. Rosemary has no plans for further changes to Badgers End and no thoughts of moving anywhere else.

Treasures

A brick-built four-bedroomed house, Treasures was constructed around 1972 by Bill Francis who had also built the two neighbouring houses – Kimego and Applewood – immediately beforehand. His widow Vera (now Martin) still lives next door at Kimego. Treasures, first called Hawthorns, was originally owned by Kenneth and Phyllis Higginson who in 1977 moved to Amersham when Kenneth, a printer, reached retirement age.

Graham and Terry Everson

Graham and Terry Everson bought the house from the Higginsons in 1977, changing the house name to Treasures – Terry's maiden surname. They have not made any structural changes to the house over the years and have no plans to do so.

Terry originates from Shepherd's Bush and Graham from the Pinner area. Terry's career was as a sales demonstrator. Graham spent many years working in the field of display and design associated with shoe companies before being employed by Aylesbury Motor Company, Luton Commercial Motors, and latterly from 1983 until 1996 by Glass's Guide as commercial editor with considerable knowledge of, and expertise in, trucks.

Before moving to Drayton Beauchamp, the Eversons had lived for thirteen years in Tring, but were attracted to Treasures as a larger, detached house with a sunny garden. They had some knowledge of the village before moving, remembering the entrance to it from the Upper Icknield Way as a "dark lane" which led straight from Tring in the days before the first roundabout was constructed at the top of the Holloway. By 1977 when they settled in the village, their three children were grown up and living away from home.

After 33 years of contented residence in the village, Terry and Graham continue to be happy here and untroubled by the slight atmosphere of isolation they believe exists. They feel very content in each other's company and have the added security of knowing that other people are nearby if needed (even if rarely seen) rather than seeking close friendships among the villagers. They see the Parish Meetings as providing a good opportunity to find out what is happening in the village and to take part in discussions about important issues affecting the village – concerns about the possibility of large Travellers' sites nearby, for instance. Their only dissatisfaction is with what they see as the Council's lack of care for the village as evidenced, for example, by the rare sweeping of the village lane and the lack of mains drainage. Graham and Terry intend to stay on in Treasures for as long as their health makes this practicable.

Kimego

By 1970 the Ballad sisters, Edith and Florence, had sold Lower Farm and were living in "The Homestead". The land between The Homestead and Badgers End traditionally belonged to Lower Farm and in the 1838 Tithe Map is marked as a grass field of four acres called Bishops Home Close which belonged to William Christopher/Jenney of Drayton Manor and was tenanted by John Parrott of Lower Farm and Morgans Farm.

In the 1960s Edie and Florrie Ballad made contact with a builder, Bill Francis, to ask him to build a bungalow which would be suitable for elderly residents with reduced mobility. Bill Francis built this bungalow, which was named Applewood, but the sisters never actually lived there, moving from The Homestead to Weston Turville instead. By a quirk of fate, Applewood was initially bought in 1972 by a couple named Beedle who had previously viewed the house in which Bill Francis was then living in Little Kingshill. Two other houses were also built alongside each other and facing the village lane on what had been the Ballads' land - Kimego and Treasures.

A four-bedroomed brick house, Kimego was built in 1971/2 by Bill Francis. At the time Bill was living in a smaller house in Little Kingshill with his wife Vera, their daughter Dawn (then fourteen), son Colin (then ten), and Vera's mother Ellen Gale. The family relocated to Kimego as soon as it was built. The name "Kimego" was chosen by the family as they had enjoyed several holidays in the west of Ireland on the edge of the Ring of Kerry when their children were small and had often passed through a village called Kimego. (That Kimego, a tiny farming and fishing community, once even had its own school, built in 1850. The building has now disappeared, but the school plaque has been set into the wall of a new building on the site.)

Bill and Vera Martin

Bill died in 1973, a year after the family moved to the village. Vera, who grew up in Ruislip, stayed on in Drayton Beauchamp although initially she had been reluctant to move to such a quiet village. For several years she was fully occupied driving the children to school in Great Missenden and continuing to work part-time in Little Kingshill. Her mother died in 1983, by which time Vera and her children were firmly settled in Drayton Beauchamp and no longer harbouring any thoughts of moving away. Vera's busy years as a young widow coping with two children and a job meant, however, that she had missed out on early opportunities to establish friendships with other villagers.

In 1986 she met her second husband, Bill Martin (a marine engineer who originates from London) when they were both working at what was then called Amersham International.

Vera and Bill have made minor modernising changes to the interior of Kimego, but have no plans for further changes. They describe themselves as self-sufficient and self-contained, happy in each other's company and busy with their interests and activities. So long as they remain healthy, able to drive, and able to manage the house and garden, they have no plans to move from the village.

Applewood

Applewood was originally a two-bedroomed bungalow built between 1970 and 1971 in the orchard of Setherwood for the Ballad sisters, Edith and Florence, although, as already mentioned, they never took up residence there. Instead, they moved to Weston Turville and sold Applewood in June 1972 to Albon and Marguerite Beedle. Applewood was designed specifically to be suitable for someone with impaired mobility, and formed part of the "infill" between Setherwood and Badgers End along with Kimego and Treasures.

John and Jean Brown 1976-2004

John and Jean Brown moved to Applewood in June 1976 from Edlesborough with their two sons Thomas and Douglas aged twelve and ten and their daughter Georgina, then seven. They were attracted to the open aspect towards the fields from the rear of the house.

The Browns carried out extensive renovations. In 1976 they adapted the existing garage to form two bedrooms and added a new garage. In 1987 they removed the entire roof from the bungalow and added an upper storey. In June 2004, with their children now adult and settled in their own homes, John and Jean sold Applewood and moved to Shropshire in search of new horizons and a fresh challenge.

Returning to Drayton Beauchamp on visits, they describe the village as now seeming closed in on itself, with hedges and trees having grown and properties having been extended so that views and open aspects have been lost.

John and Jean feel privileged to have lived in Drayton Beauchamp. They have many happy memories of friends and neighbours and describe Drayton Beauchamp as a village full of great characters and an active community life. They recall with pleasure Parish Meetings held in villagers' homes, church concerts and marvellous suppers, bonfire nights and barn dances, Silver Jubilee and VJ Day celebrations. They consider Drayton Beauchamp, in short, a wonderful place for a family to live.

David and Elisabeth Ryder 2004-

David and Elisabeth Ryder moved with their two daughters - then aged ten and six - to Applewood in 2004, having bought the house from John and Jean Brown. Before coming to the village they had lived in Aston Clinton from 1991-5 and

Cheddington from 1995-2004. David originates from Chesham and Elisabeth from Eastcote near Harrow although her parents now live only a few miles away in Eaton Bray.

They were attracted to Drayton Beauchamp because of its quietness and to Applewood because of its generous garden and views towards the Chiltern Hills. David, who runs a computer business, works from home but has an office in Aylesbury and travels around the country too. Elisabeth is very involved in charity work. They knew before moving that the village offered few social amenities and that owning a car and being able to drive were vital. (One daughter, for instance, goes by taxi to school in Aylesbury, but the other relies on Elisabeth to take her to and from school in Tring.)

Since buying Applewood, the Ryders have made a few internal changes to the layout of the rooms, but have no plans for further modifications. They themselves have no thoughts of moving away from the village where they are very happy, and they would not like it to change too much from the way it is now, seeing it as a unique place with its own somewhat quirky charm.

KIMEGO

Bill & Vera Martin

APPLEWOOD

Elisabeth & Dave Ryder & Family

THE BARN

Bob & Eve Shuttle

Setherwood

Originally comprising two "two up-two down" farm cottages which belonged to Lower Farm, Setherwood was traditionally called 1 and 2 "Ballad Cottages" or "Lower Farm Cottages". The building is believed to date from the mid-eighteenth century. The external walls are of brick - originally plain but painted cream by Bob and Eve Shuttle in the 1970s - and the roof is of clay tiles. There are two stables, wooden and with clay-tiled roofs, probably of the same age as the house. The house sits centrally in what is now a three-quarter acre plot, the front gate framed by an old damson tree, and with a well - one of the many in the village - in its front garden.

Robert and Paula Collier

Paula and her older brother Robert moved from their grandparents' home in Aston Clinton to 2 Ballad Cottages in 1944 with their parents Annie and Wallace Collier. Their grandfather owned "The Boiling Kettle" tea rooms on Aston Hill which were erected when the area was an army camp during World War I. After the camp became RAF Halton, the tea rooms were turned into a bungalow which became the Colliers' first home until Wallace was called up for service in the Royal Army Ordnance Corps in World War II. In the latter months of the war, Robert can recall his mother counting the bombers as they left for raids in Germany and then counting them back again as they returned to their base at Cheddington or Wing.

Paula and Robert (whose special friends were Robin Hillyard of Drayton Cottage and Mick Anns) enjoyed an idyllic childhood in the village free from the pressures which come from television and other modern electronic wizardry. They played unsupervised, and felt completely safe to roam across the fields to pick blackberries and wild flowers. They loved the spot behind the churchyard where violets grew by the old kissing gate and where the only sound was the singing of the birds.

Harvest time brings back happy memories of picnic lunches in the fields and of helping to rake up the stalks which had been missed when the sheaves were being made. These would then be taken home so that the chickens could feed on the grain. Before the process became mechanised, Paula and Robert remember hayricks being made with pitchforks and a horse-driven elevator. The day ended with a ride home on top of the hay cart and finally a Harvest Thanksgiving service in the village church and supper in the schoolroom nearby. Bill Oliphant held a village fireworks party every year at Morgans Farm when jacket potatoes and gingerbread were served and when each child was allowed to choose a firework from a table before taking it to a "grown-up" to light. They remember too the wonder of frost patterns on the bedroom windows and the annual Christmas party in the schoolroom. During the severe winter of 1947 the snow plough came through the village after it had been cut off for several days. The drifts which resulted seemed, to small children, to be as high as the houses on either side of the lane.

Periodically the village lane was resurfaced. An army of vehicles and men arrived. The old surface was heated to melting point by a huge burner underneath one of the vehicles. Men with shovels would follow behind, removing the melted tar and placing it in a lorry for disposal. Hot molten tar would then be poured on to the lane and shiny new grit shovelled on to the surface. The final task – and the one most enjoyed by the village children – was the smoothing of the surface by the noisy steam roller. The air was full of the acrid smell of hot molten tar and bystanders had to be careful not to end up with black tar stuck to shoes and socks.

Paula and Robert recognise that, during their carefree childhood years in the village, their mother was labouring hard to look after them as well as working full time in the family café. Doing the laundry was a particularly onerous process. The linen was boil-washed in the kitchen in the copper. This was heated by a fire lit beneath the large copper bowl, the chimney being shared with the fireplace which stood on the back wall of the living room. The laundry was then rinsed, starched, blued and mangled before being pegged out on the line using the dolly pegs which the gypsies sold to villagers. The toilet was a lean-to at the end of the house next to the lean-to barn. The well in the front garden was used as a refrigerator. Perishables such as butter or milk would be placed in a traditional glass sweet jar with a rope tied around the neck so that the jar could be lowered into the water at the bottom of the well.

During their eight years in the village the family had the kind of plain but nutritious diet which was all that was available in the early post-war years. Out-of-season fruits and vegetables were unheard-of and treats like strawberries in early summer and tangerines at Christmas could be looked forward to with particular pleasure because of their rarity. Every week basic supplies arrived in the village by van. Milk was delivered by Mr Pitkin, groceries by Nicholls of Aston Clinton, bread from a bakery in Tring, and coal from Jeffries at Marston Gate on the old Aylesbury branch line of the London and North Western Railway.

There were no buses serving Drayton Beauchamp. As a result, a visit to Tring or Aylesbury involved crossing the meadow by the church and walking along the canal to the A41 at Buckland so as to catch a bus at the "Surprise" at Bucklandwharf. The return (scary) walk was always from the top of Tring Hill, with the children holding their mother's hands very tightly, especially if the wind was blowing. The Moat House was avoided if at all possible, being by that stage a derelict and "spooky" cottage, soon to be demolished. After the children's father was demobbed and had returned home, the trip to the bus stop was made by motorbike. Their father drove, Robert sat on the tank, and their mother on the pillion with Paula in her arms.

Lottie and Walter Hedges lived in the adjoining cottage, 1 Ballad Cottages, and indeed the Hedges' daughter Peggy had been born in an upstairs bedroom there. The fireplace in this cottage was situated on the right-hand wall of the front room as viewed from the lane. Lottie Hedges did all of her cooking, baking and the heating of water on this range. Just before the Colliers left the village a septic tank was installed in the garden of number 1 in preparation for the installation of a flush toilet, but it was not yet functioning.

Paula particularly admired Lottie Hedges' long silvery white hair. She fashioned this into one very long plait which she then wound around her head and anchored with hair pins. Paula and Robert loved to be invited into the Hedges' kitchen where they were offered fresh homemade bread spread with dripping and with a pinch of salt added to "bring out the flavour".

Rent was paid to the Ballads at Lower Farm, and Paula's description of that farmhouse can be found in the Lower Farm chapter.

In 1952 the Collier family moved to Wendover to a home with running water and more space, but their eight years in Drayton Beauchamp left Paula and Robert with an abiding love of the countryside and, for Paula, with a passion for botanical painting. They believe they left their hearts in Drayton Beauchamp, and find themselves drawn back to the village each year to revisit the happy haunts of their childhood.

Edith and Florence Ballad

In December 1957 Fred Ballad, the farmer at Lower Farm, died there. His sisters Edie and Florrie sold the farm to Bill Oliphant of Morgans Farm, retaining for themselves the four cottages which had been used to accommodate their farm workers – 1 and 2 Ballad Cottages (now Setherwood) and 3 and 4 Ballad Cottages (now Badgers End).

In 1959 the two sisters moved from Lower Farm to 1 and 2 Ballad Cottages, renaming them "The Homestead". They remained there until 1971 when, as has already been described, despite having commissioned a new bungalow to be built next door for themselves (Applewood), they moved instead to Weston Turville and sold both Applewood and The Homestead. The new owners of The Homestead renamed it "Setherwood Cottage". Conversion from two cottages into one house took place but much modernisation and upgrading has been needed over the years in order to turn it into the substantial family home it is now with four bedrooms and three public rooms.

Bob and Eve Shuttle

Bob and Eve Shuttle, together with their two-year old son, moved in 1974 from Tring to Setherwood which they had bought in 1973. Their daughter was born shortly afterwards.

Bob originated from Kent and Eve from Islington. The two met when both were working for the Prudential, marrying in 1971 and living first in Kensington before moving to Tring. They wanted very much to live in a rural location, and recognised the potential of Setherwood (and of the 27' x 56' timber-framed and timber-clad barn which lay behind it) and were attracted by the five acres of land around the property and the views towards the Chilterns.

When Bob and Eve moved into Setherwood, a stable yard lay between the large barn and the house with a stable block at each end of the yard. Their predecessors at Setherwood had bred horses and therefore used all of the stable accommodation. Bob demolished one stable block and left the other which stood at the west side. He also constructed a swimming pool in the back garden in 1975, a two-storey extension at the east end of the house a year later, and he painted the external walls of the house cream. He and Eve kept Shetland ponies, and eventually bought a horse for their daughter. "Dougal" lived to a ripe and happy old age.

At one stage Bob contemplated developing the barn and demolishing Setherwood which by 1974 had already been converted from two cottages into one house, but remained in need of considerable upgrading. For instance there was still a void marking where one of the two staircases had been removed and Lottie Hedges' old range still stood in the room which Bob and Eve converted from kitchen to dining room. In the end, Bob was allowed to dismantle, move and convert the barn although this resulted in the loss of its status as a listed property. He and Eve moved into their new home in 1984, selling Setherwood (which retained around three-quarters of an acre of land) to Sue and David Whinyates.

David and Susan Whinyates

David and Sue Whinyates moved in 1984 from Halton village to Setherwood with their three daughters, then aged fourteen, twelve and nine. David originated from Swanage in Dorset and Sue from Surrey. The two met in Leatherhead and married in 1968. After various moves, a home with character and a bigger garden was decided upon, and Setherwood in Drayton Beauchamp proved the ideal location – within reasonable commuting distance for David to his work in High Wycombe as Finance Director of a pharmaceutical firm, and with a swimming pool and large garden for the girls.

The Whinyates and the Shuttles, who now lived nearby in The Barn, became good friends, and the fact that the Shuttles remained such close neighbours helped Sue and David to become acquainted with other village families and thus to feel at home quickly. Their daughters continued to attend school in Halton and then in Wendover, with one going on to Aylesbury High School. At that time, several village children attended Aylesbury schools and walked together to and from the B489 crossroads where the school bus stopped. The girls loved the village as much as their parents did, getting on well with the other local children and enjoying the Shetland ponies which Bob and Eve Shuttle kept. One of their daughters eventually acquired a horse of her own and rode regularly with the Shuttles' daughter.

Setherwood proved to require much modernising and was expensive to maintain. Sue and David carried out several major improvements to make the house comfortable and modern, with its four bedrooms, three public rooms, a large kitchen and a conservatory. They worked hard too to create an attractive garden. Sue and David firmly believe that the people in a community make it what it is. Sue became Co-ordinator of the village's Neighbourhood Watch Scheme and an attentive neighbour to those in the village who were elderly and frail. Both she and David participated enthusiastically in whatever social activities were organised locally and played a full part in village life.

When David retired and the girls had all left home, the couple decided that they should move to a smaller property which would require less expensive maintenance. They were keen to remain in a rural area, however, and particularly wanted to purchase a "converted barn with character". They found exactly what they wanted in Singleborough near Great Horwood and moved there in 2002, selling Setherwood to Diana and Melvyn Dickinson. Singleborough is a tiny hamlet of twenty or so houses along a single road with no shop, church or other public building – a smaller version of Drayton Beauchamp, perhaps, apart from the absence of a church. They are very happy there, and enjoy gardening, golf, walking, and other country pursuits.

David and Sue look back at their years in Drayton Beauchamp as a happy time in their lives which has left them with many fond and often hilarious memories. They were greatly missed when they moved away, but remain in close touch with the friends they made during their eighteen years here.

Melvyn and Diana Dickinson

Diana, who comes from Herefordshire, and Melvyn, who comes from Yorkshire, met in the 1970s when Diana was at university in Leeds. For several years the couple lived abroad in connection with Melvyn's work in sales and marketing – the Emirates, France, and Colorado, USA – but in 1997 they bought a converted barn in Little Gaddesden which was within reasonable commuting distance of Melvyn's work base in Harlow and of major airports. By 2002 his work base had changed to Henley, so the move to Drayton Beauchamp allowed their two children – by then fourteen and twelve – to remain at school in Tring while shortening Melvyn's commute a little too. Melvyn is now working in Diana's family's cider business in Herefordshire. Diana, trained as a dietician and based in the NHS for many years, later undertook additional training as a beautician, setting up her own business at Ashridge Business School. Subsequently and until recently Diana also worked in the family firm where she set up and ran an eating facility.

Diana, a "country girl", feels happy in the village and meets many neighbours during her regular walks with their dog Kes. Melvyn's long commute and frequent absences because of work have made it harder for him to integrate into the village, but the couple were made to feel very welcome by their neighbours when they were newcomers. The house and village have both suited them well at this particular time in their lives, but if they moved again in future, they would look for a village with a more active community life. They wonder if the church could be used more often for village social events, and suggested that the setting up of a periodic village newsletter – assuming that volunteers could be found to deliver it – would encourage local people to share news, would ensure that village events were widely publicised, and perhaps would also foster a greater sense of community spirit. (This, of course, has now been put into effect with the arrival of Village Life, a community magazine for the villages of Drayton Beauchamp, Aston Clinton and Buckland. The cost of producing this is borne by advertisers, and its distribution is by a band of volunteers.)

The Barn

Bob and Eve Shuttle

The Barn, clad with elm boarding and now with a peg tile roof, was listed in 1979 in the National Monuments Record as dating from the seventeenth-eighteenth century. At that time its roof was of corrugated iron. Some of the timbers used in its construction may well have come from dismantled men-o-war acquired by local farmers in exchange for the ducks and geese which they walked to market in London. Behind it is a medieval ridge and furrow field which has never been ploughed in "modern" times and whose irrigation has always been the moisture coming down from the hills.

One of the farm buildings attached to Lower Farm, this barn originally sat behind the cottages called 1 and 2 Ballad Cottages or Lower Farm Cottages (and now called Setherwood). During David Ballad's boyhood, it was used for rearing calves although further back in its history it may have been a threshing barn. In 1984, and after considerable negotiation with the Planning Department, Bob and Eve Shuttle were finally given permission to convert the now de-listed barn into a dwelling, dismantling it and reassembling it further into their field to the rear of Setherwood and at the end of a new private driveway which was constructed on the site of the former entrance to the original barn and Setherwood. The painstaking work was carried out by local builder Stanley Ward. Bob and Eve moved from Setherwood into The Barn, which sits in over three acres of land, in 1984.

When they first moved to Drayton Beauchamp in 1974, Bob and Eve were well aware that it was a quiet village lacking amenities such as gas and mains drainage, and that residents who did not drive could feel very isolated. What they had not considered was that as young newcomers it would take many months before they came to know and to be accepted by the established, rather older residents. They retained many old friends, however, and eventually put down strong roots in the village, aware that if the need arises, villagers will help each other even though they may not see each other often at other times. On the minus side, they felt sad that this quiet backwater with its lovely rural lane and no traffic had become over the years a village through which traffic speeds with impunity. They described themselves as "content" in life, actively and happily involved with their children and grandchildren and enjoying the beautiful views towards the Chiltern Hills.

Sadly, Bob died suddenly in December 2009 and Eve in March 2010. They continue to be greatly missed in the village.

Tom & Margaret Ross & Family

BEAUCHAMP BARN

THE LONG BARN

Nalini & Sanu Desai

LOWER FARM

Meryl & William Nodes & Family

Beauchamp Barn

Originally a timber-framed barn belonging to Lower Farm, this building, larger before its conversion than it is now, was one of three barns in close proximity to one another around the farmyard. All three were bought by William Oliphant from the Ballad family in 1959 and then sold by him in 1972 to Peter Joiner and Alan Sparke who, as "The Cottage Men", bought and developed derelict buildings which could be converted into homes. The firm went out of business before the other two barns, now called Long Barn and Walnut Tree Barn, had been completed. All were in a state of some dilapidation before the conversion work began but still retained some fine timbers and a framework for enlargement and conversion. In 1972 only a portion of the land behind Beauchamp Barn was sold to the Cottage Men, but the following year a further area was added to this, giving a total of just over one acre of land.

Beauchamp Barn, which may date as far back as 300 years, sits at the head of a shared driveway facing towards the village lane, with Long Barn to the side and Walnut Tree Barn opposite. The building is in the shape of a square-bottomed "U" with the original barn - probably a three-bay threshing barn but used for agricultural machinery prior to conversion - forming the base of the "U" and two "legs" added to it. In a map dated 1839 and another dated 1899, the barn already appears in the shape of a "U", but presumably the original "legs" subsequently fell down or were demolished as the current "legs" are of modern construction. The original large central bay which would have been the threshing floor extends upwards for two storeys and an upper floor was added at each end of the building during the barn's conversion. There are large entrances on either side of the central bay, one higher than the other, probably to allow a heavily-laden harvest wagon to enter. The roof would originally have been thatched. By the time of the barn's conversion, however, part of the roof was of corrugated iron and part of clay tiles, and a roof of attractive old handmade clay peg tiles was then put on the whole building. Internally there are many exposed roof trusses and rafters, the remaining original timbers complemented by newer elm timbers. The elm, oak and cherry beams which are also exposed and which form the framework of the interior walls are similarly a combination of original and new.

Maps of 1736, 1839 and 1899 show no water at all behind the barn although the two later maps show a small pond (used by the Lower Farm cattle) between the front corner of the barn and Setherwood next door. The pond (large enough for a rowing boat) which now sits behind Beauchamp Barn seems to have been dug out only in the early 1970s while the barn itself was being converted.

Maurice and Joyce Cook – 1974-82

The first residents after conversion in 1974 were Maurice and Joyce Cook who, attracted by Buckinghamshire education and the striking appearance of Beauchamp Barn itself, moved there from Northall in Bedfordshire with their two sons, then aged five and four years. The only changes they made were to construct a wall on one side of the upper floor overlooking the main living area to give privacy in the bedroom which lies behind, and in 1978 to add a small porch at the front of the barn leading into the kitchen.

Joyce and Maurice Cook found the village a place where people tended to be rather reserved, but even so they made strong friendships which have endured despite the passing of time. In 1982, wanting a smaller house, they moved to Dinton and then to Long Marston. Joyce, now widowed, currently lives in Shropshire.

Tom and Margaret Ross – 1982 –

In July 1982 Beauchamp Barn was bought by Tom and Margaret Ross who moved there with their daughter, then fourteen, and son, almost twelve. Scottish by birth, the family had lived in Vancouver, Canada from 1971-1976 before moving to Wendover and thence to Drayton Beauchamp. They were attracted to the barn because of its uniqueness, the size of the garden, and the accessibility of the village to schools, main line stations, and friends in and around Wendover. The only change they have made to the building is the addition of a wall on the upper floor above the living area to balance the wall on the opposite side which had been constructed by the Cooks.

Tom, a semi-retired consulting actuary, and Margaret, a retired counsellor, are very happy in the village and busily involved in local matters. Tom has been for many years Chairman of the Parish Meeting and Margaret is the village correspondent for the Bucks Herald as well as being the researcher and author of this Village Archive Project. With both children now grown-up and living away from home, the couple acknowledge that the barn is a large dwelling for two, but they would be reluctant to move from the area where they have lived contentedly for so long, and their yearnings for Scotland are satisfied (at least for the time being) by their ownership of a flat in Peebles, Margaret's home town.

The Long Barn

The Long Barn sits at right angles to the village lane and shares a drive with Beauchamp Barn and Walnut Tree Barn. The Long Barn was still in use as a pig barn in the 1960s and Alan Kempster remembers going there as a young boy with his twin brother to feed the pigs.

The Long Barn was bought in 1973 from Bill Oliphant by Peter Joiner and Alan Sparke of "The Cottage Men". The work of converting it into a dwelling was completed in 1975, a year after the completion of Beauchamp Barn. Among the earliest barn conversions in Aylesbury Vale, these two barns aroused considerable interest and admiration. Workmanship was of an exceptionally high standard and the proof of this remains in that the solid wood floors, doors and staircases constructed by Webster and Cannon of Aylesbury (a firm which was in existence from 1891-1987) show little evidence of wear after 35 years. The external walls of both buildings are constructed of a double layer of special breeze blocks protected by felt, batten and finally elm cladding. The roof has an aluminium lining and thick felt beneath the clay tiles.

It is not known exactly how old The Long Barn is, but the area which houses the kitchen and whose external walls are of brick dates back to the early 1800s. Above the kitchen was a hayloft in which people would have slept. A number of beams are believed to be at least six centuries old, but it is likely that some would have been brought in from other local buildings which were being demolished and some would even originally have been ships' timbers. It is highly improbable that all of the beams would have belonged to whatever may have been the first building on this site.

Sanu and Nalini Desai

The first and only owners of The Long Barn are Sanu and Nalini Desai whose initial impression of the barn was of an "empty, beautiful" building. Sanu, who until retirement worked as a Plastic Surgeon for the Oxford Health Region and Nalini, who worked as an Anaesthetist under the surname Chaubal, met in 1952 when both were medical students in Mumbai and both have now lived in the UK for over 50 years. Married in 1963, the couple have recently celebrated 45 years of living in the Aylesbury area. In the early 1980s Sanu was elected President of the Plastic Surgery Section of the Royal Society of Medicine and served on its main Council for some three years. In 1988 he became Hunterian Professor of the Royal College of Surgeons, England, for his work on cleft lip repair in the newborn. Both Sanu and Nalini retired in 1997 and, now released from the punishing work schedules of many years, are able to travel more and to enjoy their one-acre garden.

Soon after moving into The Long Barn in July 1975, the couple organised the clearing of the "garden" where the grass stood ten feet high. They demolished the huge greenhouses (120' x 60') which Bill Oliphant had had constructed and which were used for a time commercially by Mick Anns. They replaced these with a gazebo, dug a swimming pool, and put in walls and trees to protect them from the north wind. They added a porch and conservatory and converted the loft to form a storage area. They have four bedrooms (three of them en-suite) and a dressing room, a large living area with an inglenook fireplace, and an open area above it at the northwest end.

When Sanu and Nalini moved to the village, Bill and Barbara Oliphant were still living at Morgans Farm but would shortly take the name "Morgans" with them when they moved to their converted dairy/cattle shed. Their former house was renamed Old Manor Farm and sold that year to the Wrights. The Joiners were still at The Cottage, selling it two years later to the Bowdens. Karl Heinz Hormel had recently moved to the Dray House, Bob and Eve Shuttle to Setherwood and Joyce and Maurice Cook to Beauchamp Barn. The Buchanans were at Lower Farm House, to be succeeded two years later by William and Meryl Nodes and William's mother Jane. Walnut Tree Barn was still derelict and consisted of two separate buildings yet to be joined and converted by Stanley Ward after The Cottage Men went out of business. Sunningdale Farm was not yet built, its three-and-a-half acre plot still agricultural land.

Sanu and Nalini recall considerable social and neighbourly activity in the village in their early years here – for instance, Harvest Suppers at the Old Rectory, a celebration for the 25th anniversary of the Coronation, another for the wedding of Prince Charles and the Princess of Wales, and village parties in various homes where each guest brought a contribution of food for the shared meal. In winter, Gordon Nicholls of Upper Farm would clear a path with his tractor through the snow lying in the village lane, thus allowing the doctors who lived at either end of the village to drive safely to the larger roads on their way to work.

Although they now feel that they know fewer of the village's residents than they did twenty years ago, Sanu and Nalini continue to be happily settled here, and would not want to move elsewhere.

Walnut Tree Barn

Walnut Tree Barn sits opposite Beauchamp Barn and at right angles to The Long Barn, sharing a driveway with both. Originally comprising two separate barns which faced each other, both were purchased for conversion from Bill Oliphant by the "Cottage Men" in 1972, but a local builder, Stanley Ward (whose wife Evelyn still lives in Church Lane), then bought the barns after the conversion process had begun and he completed the work. The two barns, one dating from 1828 and the other from 1878, had both been farm buildings belonging to Lower Farm. In Michael Anns' childhood one was used as an open-fronted cart hovel and winter cattle shelter, and the other as stables with a hay barn above. The kitchen, built during the barn's conversion in 1979, joined these two buildings together. Although a two-storey building had been given planning approval, in the event only a one-storey, four-bedroomed home was constructed, with brick walls and a tiled roof. The only change made since construction has been to extend one bedroom to form a sitting room. No further structural changes are planned.

Barbara Thomas

David and Barbara Thomas were the first residents of Walnut Tree Barn, buying the house from Stanley Ward and moving in with their ten-year-old daughter in November 1979. At the time they lived in Bedgrove, Aylesbury, but had long wanted to live in a village. They gave the barn its name because of the walnut tree in the garden. Barbara was originally from Harrow but moved with her parents to Bromley in Kent where she met David. The two married in 1963 and lived in Bexley before moving to Buckinghamshire. David's career was as a marketing director of flag-making companies. Barbara is now retired.

The church has been important in both David's and Barbara's lives. David was a choirboy when young, and played the organ at St Mary's Church in the village for several years. He served as Churchwarden there, as did Barbara for many years. Barbara was also heavily involved in the conservation work which is essential if this ancient building is to be maintained and protected for the future.

David died in 2004 and Barbara has remained at Walnut Tree Barn. She has no plans to move house in the near future and would in any case want to stay in the area. She sees the village as a friendly, charming location which (perhaps fortunately) lacks the amenities which might otherwise encourage development and unwelcome expansion.

SETHERWOOD

David & Barbara Thomas

WALNUT TREE BARN

Lower Farm House

Serving as the farmhouse for what was once a large and thriving farm, Lower Farm House is thought to have been built around 1740 on the site of a previous building which, as so often happened in the past, burned down. John Bly the antiques expert is of the opinion that the present building may well have been designed by William Kent (1685-1748), architect and designer. It is likely to be somewhat newer than those buildings in the village which have earth floors – the Dower House, the Cottage, Upper Farm and Old Manor Farm.

Now a Grade II listed building, Lower Farm House has three reception rooms and four bedrooms. The outside walls are of traditional red brick and the steeply elevated roof is of old clay tiles. The pegs securing these tiles would originally also have been of clay, but this has been replaced by iron. Some of the sash windows still have their original glass; the wooden shutters were replaced in the 1960s. One window above the front door has been bricked up – a common way of avoiding the Window Tax which was in force from 1696 until 1851 and which was levied on houses with more than six windows.

Lower Farm House, as is the case with many other old houses in the village, sits sideways on to the village lane and facing south/southwest. There are only two windows on the east side. One intriguing explanation may be that this design reflects the old belief in a "Plague Wind" blowing from the direction of London. By building houses to face in the opposite direction, it would have been hoped to avoid the deadly effects of this wind. A more prosaic explanation offered by the local farmer is that farmhouses were built sideways to the road so as to maximise the space and to ensure that the living room would face the courtyard and farm buildings. This allowed the farmer to keep an eye on the work of the farm whilst he himself remained dry and sheltered.

Lower Farm House and the Rectory are the only two buildings in the lower part of the parish with a cellar. In the case of Lower Farm House, the original cellar floor was of old brick and the steps which now lead from the cellar up to the kitchen are of brick edged with timber. A very old safe, inscribed "Hamilton & Co., London" is cemented to the cellar floor. During the Ballad family's ownership of Lower Farm, the usual access to the cellar was by means of a wide flight of steps which descended from where the door to the study now stands towards the end of the building. The high-ceilinged cellar was used constantly and cooking may even have been done there. Butter was churned in this cellar and salted pigs were stored there. Outside, big old oak trees grew in the paddock behind the farm and the family often enjoyed rook pie thanks to the birds which nested in these trees.

The back door led straight into the kitchen, a large rectangular room which, with its generously proportioned farm table, was the family's main gathering place.

The two "front rooms" were used only for special visitors and never by the family. In the early years of the building's life, however, farm servants would probably have been confined to the back of the house, leaving the farmer and his family to enjoy these lighter rooms at the front. A mysterious trapdoor set into the kitchen ceiling opens in what is now an upstairs bedroom.

Paula and Robert Collier, whose parents were tenants of number 2 Ballad Cottages from 1944-52 (paying 10s a week rent) remember as children visiting the farmhouse where the door was always left open. Chickens frequently strayed into the kitchen and had to be chased outside. Tomatoes ripened on the kitchen windowsills and apple rings for winter use were dried on strings at the windows. A dense grape vine covered the front of the building. Grapes were dried hanging from rafters in the kitchen, and a large grandfather clock ticked majestically in the "parlour". As a treat the tenants' children would be allowed to watch chickens hatching in the incubator.

Lower Farm House sits on a mound with steps leading up to the front door and steps down to the kitchen. Outside there is a Victorian toilet and a shed with old timber beams. The property sits in three-and-a-half-acres of land which consists of three paddocks and a garden shared with the tiny cottage which is situated at the side of the farmhouse and which is described separately. If, as is believed, this cottage was originally used as a dairy, this tends to confirm the idea that an older farmhouse stood, perhaps two centuries earlier, on the site of the current farmhouse. There are no fewer than four wells close to the farmhouse – essential, no doubt, given the number of animals and people requiring water when the farm was a large, busy concern. Intriguingly, the Drayton Lodge Estate archive includes a receipt dated 1918 for repairing one of the well pumps, and one dated 1915 for the cost of re-glazing the window of the "brew house" at Lower Farm. Whether the cottage was used as a brew house or whether this was another of the farm's outbuildings is not now known. The previous year, the stable and part of the "middle barn" at Lower Farm were re-thatched. It seems likely that these were the buildings later converted into Walnut Tree Barn. In 1898 the estate inventory lists a wash house, meal house, wood house and granary among the farm buildings.

Lower Farm in 1838 was owned by William Christopher/Jenney of Drayton Manor. The farmer was John Parrott who also farmed Manor/Morgans Farm. Lower Farm at that stage shared over 475 acres with Manor Farm and had four farm cottages of its own – now called Setherwood and Badgers End. By 1851 Thomas Rodwell was farming Lower Farm and 230 acres. The Rodwell family continued to farm there as tenants of Stewart William Jenney for over fifty years, with Maria Rodwell, a single woman aged 44, appearing in the 1901 Census as the farmer. In the 1911 Census, Walter Ball, his wife Elizabeth and four children are listed as living at Lower Farm where Walter was working as farm bailiff. The Ball family seem to have remained there until at least 1918. By 1914 there was little money left to run the Jenney estates and every expense was carefully checked and often queried. In that spirit, a letter of that year raises the notion that it would be financially wiser for tax purposes to classify Lower Farm House as a house rather than as a farmhouse.

In October 1919 Lower Farm was sold by the Jenney estate to Joseph Purssell Ballad (grandfather of David Ballad of Rye Hill Farm). The Ballad family remained at Lower Farm for the next forty years. The farmlands extended to over 195 acres from the canal bridge at Puttenham at one end all the way to the far side of the two farm cottages now known as Badgers End at the other, and included barns, stables, outbuildings and four cottages. Until Bill Oliphant bought Lower Farm from David's family in 1959, Gordon and David helped extensively with the work of Lower Farm. In those days farming was very labour-intensive and most of the slaughtering of animals and birds was carried out at the farm itself. David can just remember there being horses at Lower Farm, David's uncle Fred Ballad being the last farmer in the area to use them. David recalls that his Aunt Florrie was for a time a teacher in Berkhamsted, while Edie always stayed at home and carried out the chores which would normally have fallen to the farmer's wife. Their brother Fred was a quiet, unassertive man. None of the three ever married.

There were several large dilapidated barns around the farmyard. All were owned by Lower Farm and most had tin roofs, although the one now known as Beauchamp Barn (used for hay and corn) may have had a slate roof. The main entrance to these barns was beside what is now Long Barn, then a pig barn. Behind lay a "baulk" - a raised strip of unploughed land with a furrow running along at either side where cows would stand to be milked.

In 1959, two years after the death of Fred Ballad, his sisters Edie and Florrie sold the farmhouse to William Oliphant (perhaps in the name of Argentum Property Investments Ltd). By this stage the farm lands had been broken up and sold and Lower Farm was no longer a working farm. Its four cottages were also sold independently and soon converted into two bigger houses. Sir John and Lady Elizabeth Guillum Scott moved in 1960 to Lower Farm House from the Old Rectory where they had been tenants, and in 1974 sold the house to Hugh and Nony Buchanan. The present owners, Meryl and William Nodes, bought the farmhouse, adjoining cottage and three quarters of an acre of land from the Buchanans in 1977. At a later stage they were able to buy two further paddocks from Bill Oliphant, giving them the current total of three-and-a-half acres of land.

William and Meryl Nodes

William and Meryl originally met as teenagers and married in 1976. Meryl worked in advertising and William in the timber trade – a job which involved considerable travel both in the UK and abroad. They moved to Drayton Beauchamp from Stanmore, attracted to a property which offered adjacent but self-contained accommodation in the "Bothy" (as the nearby cottage was then called) for William's widowed mother, Jane. The village met William's requirement of being within commuting distance by car of Clapton where he was employed as a sales director, and the garden delighted Jane. Meryl, a city-lover, felt somewhat isolated until she learned to drive shortly before their son, born three months before they moved to the village, started school. Jane died in November 2000.

As Lower Farm House is a listed building, there are major restrictions on the changes which can be made. Meryl and William have merely replaced the concrete kitchen floor with quarry tiles, and the kitchen cupboards with a wooden farmhouse dresser.

The couple are very happy in the village and see it as a friendlier place than it was in the early years of their residence, with more community spirit and more feeling of villagers working together. They cite as examples the annual village "litterblitz", the Buckland and Drayton Preservation Alliance (BADPA) campaign to minimise the adverse effects of the A41 bypass, the Neighbourhood Watch Scheme, and the higher attendance at Parish Meetings in recent years. Meryl and William are themselves very involved in activities which benefit Drayton Beauchamp, helping with local events and keeping a watchful eye on older, more vulnerable residents. Meryl has held the position of Clerk to the Parish Meeting since 1981, a post which has become progressively much more complex and time-consuming over the years, but one which is absolutely vital to the village. Interestingly, Sir John Guillum Scott was Chairman of the Parish Meeting for eighteen years until 1973 and Hugh Buchanan served as Clerk to the Parish Meeting for three years. This means that for over fifty years a resident of Lower Farmhouse has served the Parish Meeting in an official capacity. A previous Clerk, W H Mayne, asked to resign from his duties in 1947 after 35 years, but his resignation was not accepted and he was obliged to continue until he died in harness in 1951.

The couple are delighted that Drayton Beauchamp still has a working farm and is a rather old-fashioned village without the modern amenities which might spoil rather than enhance its character. At the same time, they feel that the appearance of the village would be improved if the unsightly overhead electricity cables were hidden and if some long-term solution appropriate to the rural setting could be found for the collapsing, unstable verges. They would like to continue to live in Drayton Beauchamp for as long as is practicable, but recognise that residents of Lower Farm House need to be able-bodied if they are to maintain the house and grounds.

Lower Farm House Cottage

This cottage, formerly called the "Bothy", is a building of considerable age and of brick and timber construction. It sits close to Lower Farm House under whose Grade II listing it is included, and shares its entrance and gardens. It is believed to have served originally as a dairy for the farm. Within living memory it served as a one-storey barn, considerably larger than it is now, and with a steeply pitched roof. A black-boarded section at the rear perhaps even joined up with what is now Long Barn, and may during the Ballads' time have been used as a place in which their pigs were killed.

The cottage was converted into a dwelling in the 1970s and has two bedrooms, a kitchen/dining room and a conservatory. The replacement in 2006 of the conservatory which was originally constructed in 1977 is the only change which has been made in recent years to the cottage. Since 2006 it has been lived in by the son, daughter-in-law and, from June 2009, the grandson of the owners of Lower Farm House.

Oliver and Zamira Nodes

Oliver Nodes was three months old when he moved with his parents to Lower Farm House in 1977. He works in Aylesbury as an IT manager dealing with offshore IT business in India. In 2001 he met Zamira who was born and brought up in Buckinghamshire. Until the birth of baby Harry, Zamira was employed as customer services manager for a large store belonging to one of the major supermarket chains.

Oliver and Zamira love living in Drayton Beauchamp and would not want to live elsewhere. Zamira describes the village as a friendly, supportive place where help in a crisis can always be counted upon. The reliable and reassuring presence so close at hand of Oliver's parents (with Zamira's own family only a little further away) has proved to be of enormous help.

The only difficulty which Zamira has noted regarding life in the village has been the practical one of negotiating stiles and kissing gates while carrying a baby in a harness or pushing a baby in a buggy.

Sunningdale Farm

Sunningdale Farm was built in stages in the 1980s by Colin Farnham, a builder who lived in a caravan in the garden during the house's construction. The land on which the house sits was traditionally a grass field of just over three acres belonging to Lower Farm and called "Corn Close". At one side of it was "Calf's Close", a one-acre grass field, and at the other side a three-acre arable field called "Ninelands". In 1919 Corn Close was sold by Stewart William Jenney to the Ballad family as part of the Lower Farm estate. Ownership then transferred to William Oliphant who bought Lower Farm in 1959 from the Ballads but Corn Close was sold in 1970 to Myra Lear who presumably then sold it to Colin Farnham. The land now extends to just over four acres with paddocks and an area of formal garden. The house itself is brick-built with a tiled roof and originally had four bedrooms, three public rooms and a large kitchen/family room. A modern stable block nearby has planning permission for conversion to living accommodation.

Colin and Diane Farnham lived at Sunningdale Farm from the time of its completion in 1987 until 1998, when it was sold - already empty but along with an aged horse still living in the field - to its present owner, Lee Seagrave.

Lee Seagrave

Lee has had to carry out significant upgrading to the house, and has extended the shoulder-height storage area above the integral garage to form an additional bedroom. Outside, he has removed an old metal barn which had collapsed and has recently replaced a second derelict barn. What purpose these barns used to serve is not known, nor even who owned them, but both seem to have been used for storage - car parts in the small barn and ancient bales of hay in the larger one. Lee would like to create an attractive garden and probably to rent out the field, perhaps to someone with horses. He would also like to encourage the water to flow at the end of the front garden alongside the village lane where the stream mysteriously collects without moving.

Lee, who was born in Kilburn, lived in Watford before moving to Drayton Beauchamp. His first wife wanted to keep horses, hence the attraction of the land which came with Sunningdale Farm. He has three children - a girl and boy aged eighteen and sixteen respectively who live with their mother in Harlow, and a seven-year old daughter living in Newbury with her mother. Lee, a plumber and gas engineer, has maintained his client base around Watford but is gradually building up local contacts. His partner is Lesley Barnett, an Aylesbury native who lives in Aston Clinton. Lesley has two adult sons still living at home and she works part-time as well as attending a photography course at Aylesbury College.

Lee has not found it particularly easy to make friends in the village. Living in the very last property before the houses give way to fields and at some distance from the nearest houses (Lower Farm House and The Cottage), he has felt geographically rather isolated. This feeling has been accentuated by the fact that he is considerably younger than many of the other residents of the village and that his work has taken him away from the village for long hours each day. Lee loves Sunningdale Farm, however, in spite of having had to fight very hard to meet the expenses of keeping it, and wants to become part of the village community. He believes strongly that the church, as the only public building, ought to be used more as the hub for village social activities, secular as well as religious, to bring people together. Lodging a copy of this Archive Project in the church would, he believes, emphasise that this is **our** village and our village's history. He suggests too that it would help newcomers if the names of houses, their residents and their telephone numbers were written on an A4-sized line drawing of the village (based on an OS map or the Google Earth map of the village) for circulation purely within the village.

Bates' Boatyard, Puttenham

Jeremy Bates and Lisa Brooks

In 1994 Jem Bates bought an acre of land at Puttenham Bottom Lock from Stephen Hill who had previously owned Lock Cottage. This land lies along the bank of the Aylesbury Arm of the Grand Union Canal. Three years later Jem launched the first boat. The shape and gentle incline of the field, created when the construction of the canal chopped the corner off a larger field, make it an ideal place for slipping 72 foot boats sideways into and out of the water. The location too is excellent, with quick access to the main line of the Grand Union Canal.

In the 1838 Tithe Map and Apportionment Document, this field - or a segment of it - is called "Three Corners". Owned by William Christopher/Jenney of Drayton Manor, it was listed as arable land and was being rented from the Jenneys by John Parrott. By 1872 the field (described in Jenney estate papers as including a "wharf"), was being rented by the tenant farmer of Draytonmead Farm which, although very close to Puttenham, still fell within the parish boundaries of Drayton Beauchamp (and was named "Draytonmead" because of this) until 1886 when it was transferred to Buckland parish. By 1905 the farmhouse was derelict and was sold along with the surrounding land by Stewart William Jenney in 1917. It seems feasible that at this point the "Three Corners" field was sold to the Grand Junction Canal Company, and then sold again in 1983 by British Waterways to Stephen Hill when he bought Lock Cottage.

Jem was born in Leighton Buzzard to parents who were both teachers. After leaving school he travelled for two years, hiking in the wilderness areas of North America, before returning to take an English degree at Warwick University. He found his life's work while reading Tom Rolt's 1944 book -"Narrow Boat" - about the restoration of an old wooden working boat called "Cressy" and its journey along the then much-neglected waterways of Britain. Jem cannot now imagine doing any other kind of work.

Jem builds new wooden canal boats of individuality and character as well as restoring and repairing existing boats. Initially he carried out boatbuilding on a mobile basis, moving with a steam box from one dry dock to another. Nowadays he owns the lease on the dry dock at Bulbourne, located at the top lock of the Marsworth Flight of the Grand Union Canal, as well as the sideslip yard at Puttenham, working on one or two boats at Bulbourne at a time and one or two at Puttenham. Among the unusual boats he has worked on are "Peary", an icebreaker dating back to 1912, with wooden sides clad in iron, and also one of the last World War II RAF rescue boats ("RAF 441"). Work has also been carried out for the National Trust on one of the last surviving Wey Barges, "Reliance".

In the hands of skilled craftsmen, boats which are 75-100 years old can be painstakingly restored so as to ensure that they will last at least as long again and still remain faithful to the original lines. Trees are selected in as environmentally friendly a way as possible (using wind-blown oaks, for instance) and seasoned for two years before work begins. This work is carried out by Jem himself and a dedicated team of skilled craftsmen with many years of experience among them as well as by newcomers who are keen to learn the skills required for the work - skills which will be transferable to other areas of work. Jem is the only full-time restorer in the country. A handful of other restorers work part-time or are based in charitable organisations.

Jem is proud to be continuing the traditions which would otherwise be lost, the 1950s having seen the end of the era of wooden boat construction by particular families specialising in building particular types of boat. He enjoys passing on his skills, arranging educational visits for schoolchildren, offering work experience placements for young people, and giving talks at places like the National Maritime Museum, the Ellesmere Port Museum, and local History Societies. He recognises his work to be important and worthwhile - the antithesis to mass production and poor workmanship - and is known throughout the country for his expertise and experience.

Over the years, Jem has had to work hard to safeguard the future of the Puttenham boatyard and to overcome the planning restrictions which would otherwise have required it to be dismantled within a very short time of his death. Fittingly, he himself lives on a canal boat with his partner Lisa and their young daughter Joselyn who was born at the boatyard.

Lock Cottage

Lock Cottage, sometimes called Lock House in old records, is situated at the side of the Grand Union (formerly Grand Junction) Canal, Aylesbury Branch. This Branch is six miles in length; Lock Cottage sits two miles from Marsworth and four miles from Aylesbury. Its official position is at Puttenham Bottom Lock, Bridge 7, Lock 11.

The cottage has a Hertfordshire address but is actually in Buckinghamshire and within the boundary of the parish of Drayton Beauchamp. The county boundary crosses the canal twice. One of the triangles of rough land between the canal and the boundary is filled with clay, presumably left there to be used by workmen repairing the canal. This clay would have had to be reached by working barge as the site is not accessible by road. It is possible that the canal company even made its own bricks as so many would have been needed.

Started in late 1809 under the Grand Junction Canal Act of 1794, the Aylesbury Branch was completed in January 1815 and Lock Cottage was built between 1813 and 1814 using, as was customary, materials left over from the building of the canal. Indeed, beams stamped "Grand Junction Canal" have been used as roof beams in the cottage.

The Baptismal Records held by St Mary's Church, Drayton Beauchamp, record the baptism on 31st August, 1815 of two children (ages not given) living at "New Canal Lock" - the earliest mention of this cottage found so far in local records. In contrast to this happy event, it is believed that a small child living at Lock Cottage many years ago drowned by falling into the canal. This may be documented in the records of Puttenham Church as the only record in the Drayton Beauchamp Church Burial Register is of a little boy aged six who was said to have lived at Little Tring and who drowned in the canal in 1860. As no indication is given about the location of this accident, however, and as addresses in old parish documents are notoriously inaccurate, it is possible that this is indeed the same child, but further research would be needed to establish this. In 1882, the village Burial Register records that the fifteen-year old son of the lock-keeper died of tetanus after having his fingers jammed in the shafts of a cart he was unloading.

From 1903 until at least 1912 Lock Cottage was lived in by David and Alice Rance and their children whose baptisms are recorded in the church's Baptismal Register. Alice was a daughter of Joseph and Esther Kempster of Drayton Beauchamp and David an Army pensioner turned lock-keeper.

Lock Cottage is a Grade II listed building - as are the canal bridge, opened in 1812, and the lock itself. The cottage is of colourwashed brick with a slate roof and a fine oriel window on the upper level. Two bedrooms and a lounge "upstairs" facing the canal are on the same level as the canal towpath, while the large family kitchen/dining room and small study downstairs are at natural ground level. The property is prone to flooding and residents must learn to recognise and to respond quickly to the early warning signs of water gathering outside on the patio, swirling in the pond, and so on. Having a lifelong interest in canals means that the current owner understands what is happening when flooding is imminent, so the situation can be managed. Magnificent views across the fields towards Whipsnade in one direction and Coombe Hill in the other compensate for the disadvantages of the cottage's sometimes rather watery location. As is the case with so many properties in the village, Lock Cottage has its own well in the garden.

Lock-keepers employed by the Grand Union Canal (which was formed in 1929 and 1932 by the amalgamation of many old canals, nationalised in 1948, and finally brought under the control of British Waterways in 1962) would traditionally have lived in Lock Cottage with responsibility for looking after both Bottom Lock Number 11 and Top Lock Number 10 where there is no cottage. Busy commercial waterways in their heyday, canals were badly affected by the increasing use of railways to transport goods, and later by the building of trucks capable of carrying large and heavy loads. Commercial use of the Aylesbury Branch declined until the time came when Lock Cottage was no longer required for lock-keepers and gradually fell into disrepair. In 1983 the Hill family are believed to have bought the cottage at auction from British Waterways. They spent several years renovating it – installing electricity and a mains water supply in the process - before selling Lock Cottage in 1990 to John and Sheila Barron.

John and Sheila Barron

John and Sheila moved into Lock Cottage in 1991, by which time their three sons were adult and living in their own homes.

John, who originates from North London and Sheila, who was brought up in Surrey, met in 1960 in Cork where both were on holiday with their respective friends - John travelling by gipsy caravan as his friend had not wanted the canal holiday which John had planned. The two married and set up home in Cockfosters where John had a motor company and Sheila looked after the company books. They retired in 1999.

John has had a keen interest in canals since boyhood, and the couple discovered Lock Cottage on one of their many walks to explore stretches of canals. They are extremely happy in the cottage, enjoying the solitude of the setting despite changes which have occurred in the eighteen years of their residence and which inevitably affect this solitude – the opening of a canal boat repair yard on one side, the addition of accommodation at the stables on the other, and the floodlighting of industrial estates which pierces the night sky.

John and Sheila have absolutely no feeling of isolation living at Lock Cottage. They have family and many friends both locally and further afield, they have a close connection with Puttenham where John is a Churchwarden, and Sheila enjoys the camaraderie of the Women's Institute. They believe that there is a strong community spirit in the area and cannot imagine that they will ever want to leave Lock Cottage.

LOCK COTTAGE

John & Sheila Barron

THE COTTAGE

Isabel & David Ogden & Family

OLD MANOR FARM

Sandy & Andrew Strain

The Stables

The Stables, a "Therapeutic Horsemanship and Western Riding Centre", is situated to the west of the B489 beyond the lower part of Drayton Beauchamp and on the narrow road leading to Puttenham. A conventional riding school used to sit on the same site, but had been closed for around two months before the current tenants rented the seven/eight acre space three years ago from landlord Malcolm Miles. Land adjoining it is used by Mr Miles for cattle, and the nearest neighbours are Lock Cottage and Bates' Boatyard.

Debbie La-Haye and her partner Dave Johnson met ten years ago through a shared interest in working with horses. They and their six-year-old son live at The Stables in a mobile home owned by Mr Miles and allowed for their use in return for help with his cattle. Debbie comes from Linslade and Dave from Northampton. Before coming to Drayton Beauchamp they lived at Cheddington where they recognised the therapeutic value of horses in work with adults with mental health problems. Keen to put their vision into practice and to develop their ideas independently, they decided to set up their own Centre. Similar work is being carried out in various parts of the United States, and Debbie and Dave keep in close touch with these organisations via the Internet, but in the United Kingdom the organisation closest in its philosophy is the new National Care Farms Initiative. As a member of this group, Debbie recently attended a reception at Highgrove House where His Royal Highness Prince Charles spoke about his strong belief in this type of work.

The philosophy behind "Horses Helping People" is that horses can be partners in therapeutic work with all kinds of disadvantaged people, both children and adults. Those coming to The Stables include children diagnosed as being on the autistic spectrum, children with cerebral palsy, adults with addiction issues, depression and other mental health problems, and carers for others. Some come for training before working in similar Centres, and there are Open Days and sponsored weekends. Mature volunteers able to work alongside the clients are carefully chosen by Debbie and Dave.

There are currently ten horses at The Stables, all hand-picked for particular traits and qualities. Horses, Debbie and Dave firmly believe, quickly pick up a person's emotional mood and energy level. Observing how horses behave and communicate, how they maintain boundaries, how assertive or submissive they are, and so on, teaches valuable lessons to vulnerable individuals who are wrestling with similar issues. Mental wellbeing can be enhanced by the calming effect of stroking a horse and by the realisation that one can communicate with, and manoeuvre, such a large animal. Actually riding the horses is only one part of what happens at The Stables.

Clients are referred to Horses Helping People by clinical psychologists, Social Services Departments, schools, General Practitioners, and other agencies. Some refer themselves or a family member. Goals may be set in advance by a client, and compared with the goals which the referrer may hope the client will achieve. What happens in each session is tailored to the needs of the individuals attending. Some clients are funded by their Local Authority, so a twelve-week course consisting of two or three hours each week is a useful guide, although open-ended work is also offered. A group of four is considered ideal, but a slightly larger group can be worked with if divided in two.

Horses Helping People is not a charitable organisation, but rather a "Community Interest Company" which is required to run as a sustainable business, reinvesting any profits in the business. Some funding is, however, available, and generous help has been given by the Aylesbury Vale Community Chest and the European Social Fund, among others.

After three years of experience in running the Centre, Debbie and Dave began to feel limited by the frustrating constraints of their current location and were keen to own a Centre in perhaps twenty acres, with woodland, an orchard, hay meadow, bigger vegetable gardens, riding trails, and an indoor school in which clients could ride during the winter months. Although sad to leave their excellent landlord, they began actively looking for land appropriate to their needs. This they have now found close to Mentmore, still in Aylesbury Vale and offering twenty-two acres where they can put their vision into practice.

So far as the village of Drayton Beauchamp is concerned, Dave and Debbie see it as a lovely, unspoilt hamlet, an oasis in a busy world and a throwback to what Buckinghamshire villages used to be like. They would not want to see it developed or "improved" in any way which would spoil its present appearance. During their time in the parish, however, they themselves have felt closer, both emotionally and geographically, to Long Marston and Puttenham because of the location of The Stables and their son's school.

The Cottage

The Cottage, also known in the past as "The Cott" or "The Thatch", is believed to date from around 1620 based on the evidence of a particular notch carved into a beam in the main room. Originally built as a single dwelling - a typical small Buckinghamshire farmhouse - The Cottage seems to have been divided internally in two by 1838. The Tithe Map of that year does not show a clear division in what appears to be a building which is larger than the one now standing, but the accompanying Tithe Apportionment Document lists William Christopher/Jenney as owner and two families as resident there - those of John Stratford and William Lovett. John Stratford is said to have a cottage and garden amounting to sixteen perches, while William Lovett has a cottage with a garden and orchard around it, as well as a strip of land higher up the village beyond the bridge over the canal – a total of just over one acre. William Lovett is listed in the censuses from 1841 until 1861, and his burial in the village churchyard is recorded in the church Burial Register in 1862 when he was "95 years and two months". He is likely to be the same William Lovett as is listed in the 1798 Buckinghamshire Posse Comitatus. William Lovett's son Joseph is listed in Kelly's Directory of 1854 as being a "carrier to Aylesbury on Saturdays". A member of the same family, the unfortunate Ann Lovett ("Widow Lovett"), found herself evicted in 1914 from her half of The Cottage for non-payment of rent of 1s 6d per week. Her goods were seized and sold, and she herself was removed to the Workhouse.

In 1914 the Jenney estate papers record that it was necessary to net the cottages to prevent birds from damaging the new thatch. When William Jenney's son Stewart William Jenney sold much of his estate in October 1919, The Cottage was sold as part of Morgans/Manor Farm to Leonard Lewin who had been living at Morgans Farm as tenant farmer from 1914. In 1921 Leonard Lewin sold Morgans Farm, The Cottage and five other farm cottages to Leslie William Webb. The estate was put up for auction in June 1925 on the instructions of Leslie Webb who had emigrated earlier that year to Windhoek, southwest Africa, to work as a farmer. It did not sell and a second auction was held in July 1926. It would seem that The Cottage still remained unsold until 11th October of that year when Leslie Webb's representative sold it to James Moor Long, a retired bootmaker of Top o' the Hill, Chesham Bois. James Moor Long in turn sold The Cottage the following day to George MacDonald Brown, the new purchaser of Manor Farm. In December 1949 William Oliphant bought Manor Farm and The Cottage from the estate of George MacDonald Brown who had died in 1944. From then until 1968 The Cottage seems to have been used mainly as accommodation for farm workers and farm managers employed at Morgans Farm.

It is believed that there have been several changes to The Cottage over the years both externally and internally. In the "Mapp of the Mannour of Drayton Beauchamp" dated 1736, The Cottage is shown as an L-shaped house, but in maps from 1824 onwards a sizeable rectangular building can be seen jutting out at right angles to the rear of the basic L-shape and coloured on the map in the same shade as the rest of the cottage, suggesting that it was part of the tenants' accommodation. The contrasting shading on the 1877 Ordnance Survey map, however, suggests that it had become a farm building by this stage rather than a dwelling. This section of The Cottage has now disappeared and the building has reverted to an L-shape. The front door opens on to the side of the chimney breast and the main room, but it is known that doorways have been blocked and staircases repositioned over the years. Two staircases would presumably have been essential when the building was used as two cottages to allow separate access for each family to its own bedrooms upstairs, but one had been removed by 1968 when Peter and Jill Joiner bought the property. A second staircase has again been built at some stage since the Joiners sold The Cottage in 1977.

A brick bread oven with a clay tile floor remains in excellent condition in the kitchen wall, as are the two large fireplaces with their original chimney stacks. A second bread oven in the fireplace of the main living room has at some time since 1977 been removed and the cavity bricked over. Charred timbers upstairs suggest that there was once a significant chimney fire which must have started in this main room downstairs. Hooks suspended from the beams in one of the bedrooms would probably have been used to hang meat - perhaps sides of pork from the pure Berkshire pigs which were reared on several of the local farms. The north wall of the house and part of the back wall (both much thicker than the single brick construction of other parts of the house) are believed to be the original timber and brick, and some of the windows are also original to The Cottage. A well still sits outside the front door and was the only source of water when the two cottages were put up for auction in 1926. The timbers of the house are likely to have come from other old buildings rather than from ships. The Cottage is one of only two homes in the village which have retained their thatched roofs, and it was given a Grade II listing in 1985 after examination by the National Monuments Record Inspector.

Betty Kempster

For at least fifteen years until 1938 members of the Ball and Kempster families lived side by side in The Cottage and enjoyed the closest of friendships.

Betty Sylvia Kempster, born in 1936, was the youngest child of Jim (born 1899 in Wingrave) and Annie (born Annie Taylor in 1900) Kempster. The other children were Aubrey (born 1920), James (1925), Doris (1927), and twins Geoffrey Thomas and Gerald William (1930). The twins were always known by their middle names, Tom and Bill, and both married girls called Betty! Aubrey was born in Barwick, Hertfordshire, his mother's home town; the others were all born in Drayton Beauchamp.

Jim Kempster came to work on a farm (presumably Morgans Farm) in Drayton

Beauchamp and first appears on the Electoral Register of 1923. Annie too came to work in the village, in her case as a Land Army Girl, and first appears on the Electoral Registers in 1930 as Annie Kempster. Jim and Annie were given the tenancy of one half of The Cottage, at that time known as Morgans Farm Cottages. Betty was born in The Cottage. Years later one of her brothers told her that on 4th July 1936, the children had all been given money to go to a fête or fair and told not to come back until it was dark. On their return, they discovered that not only had the cat and guinea pig had babies, but their mother had also given birth to their new baby sister in an upstairs bedroom.

Next door in the cottage nearest the crossroads were Mick Anns' grandparents, Amy and Edgar Ball with their children Margery, Sylvia and Billy. Betty was named after Sylvia who was her godmother. Annie and Margery were the closest of friends and the two families constantly helped each other. Billy Ball was very fond of Annie and was always happy to be left in her care if his mother was busy with other chores. As there were six children including twins in one family and three, including Billy who could not walk and needed a wheelchair, in the other, the walk to Tring for either family to do shopping must have been a considerable expedition. Taking turns to shop and to look after each other's children would have made the undertaking much easier.

In 1938 the Kempster family left the village when they were allocated a Council house at Bucklandwharf and Betty's father secured work as a storeman at Halton Camp. Although she was still very small when her family moved away, the link with the village was maintained as Wally Kempster visited frequently to see the twins and Betty can remember Wally teaching her as a small girl to say his name in pidgin Italian when he returned home from Italy after the war. (Wally's family and Betty's are closely related by a double link between both of Betty's paternal great-grandparents and both of Wally's paternal grandparents.)

Betty would regularly be brought back by her mother to visit their friends and former neighbours, the Balls. Betty often came back to the village by herself too to ride a horse owned by Jenny Brown, daughter of Captain Brown at Morgans Farm, while Jenny Brown rode her mother's horse. Betty would then have to walk back home to Bucklandwharf via the churchyard in the dusk, a walk she described as "creepy" but worth it for the pleasure of riding a horse. This friendship seems to have lasted until Jenny moved from the area when Betty was fourteen or so.

In 1970 Betty married Philip Leslie Kempster – one of the "Tring Kempsters" – thus retaining her maiden name. Their five children still live within 25 miles of Drayton Beauchamp. Betty and Phil have lived in Wales for 21 years but are now keen to move back to where their roots are. Betty is very proud to have "Drayton Beauchamp" recorded as her birthplace on her birth certificate and passport.

Simon and Jill Joiner

In 1968 Peter and Jill Joiner bought The Cottage (at that time still known as "The Cott") from Bill Oliphant, moving in with their daughter Katherine (Kate) aged three and their son Simon aged two. Lucy was born in 1970 and Sophie in 1971.

The Joiners carried out a considerable amount of renovation at The Cottage, adding a cloakroom and lobby beside the kitchen and constructing a brick garage in 1972. There are now three reception rooms and four bedrooms in The Cottage as well as extensive attics under the thatched roof. The gardens extend to two-thirds of an acre, with views to Mentmore Towers in the distance.

The family consider The Cottage as the loveliest and most special of all the homes in which they have lived, and Drayton Beauchamp as an idyllic place for children. Simon vividly remembers a "scary rope swing" which hung from a tree over the empty canal behind the church, an area which was a favourite spot for the village children to gather. He recalls also an occasion on which his sister almost burned down the new garage built by their father beside The Cottage when she was playing with matches. The family held legendary parties on the Friday of every August Bank Holiday weekend with guests' cars parked all the way through the village and spilling into the nearby field. The Temperance Seven provided the musical entertainment on one occasion. After the annual party, Peter and his Morgan car club friends would race that weekend at Silverstone. Occasionally Jill used to take the children to their primary school in Aston Clinton in a governess trap pulled by their pony mare Polly. Polly gave birth to her foal Sukie in the garden of The Cottage.

Simon and Kate took part in a great deal of professional child photographic modelling, almost always in London. One set of photographs, however, was taken in the garden of The Cottage and featured Sophie as the dairymaid in A A Milne's poem "The King's Breakfast". Kate was featured as the Queen and Simon as the King. The photos were produced in the shape of a mock slice of bread and were shown on the television programme "Blue Peter".

Peter and his friend Alan Sparke set up "The Cottage Men" - a firm which bought dilapidated properties and converted them into comfortable homes. In Drayton Beauchamp they purchased from Bill Oliphant three barns - now Beauchamp Barn, Long Barn and Walnut Tree Barn. Simon remembers exploring the building site with his father during the barn conversions, watching the huge pond being dug behind Beauchamp Barn, and climbing the high mounds of mud.

The Joiners moved away from the village in 1977, settling first in Winslow where they created Scrummys Restaurant following their success at outside catering which had begun when, as Scrummydumptious Catering, they once or twice provided food at parents' evenings to raise funds for Aston Clinton School. Their next adventure was in Apsley Guise where they restored the Holt Hotel and introduced jazz sessions in the "C'est La Bas" cellar bar there (Peter being an avid jazz enthusiast). Their final move in the UK was to Cropredy near Banbury where they owned a plot of land on the South Oxford Canal. They had two large narrow boats and a living wagon (of the type which used to be pulled behind steam rollers and used like a caravan). This wagon was greeted with excited admiration by Fred Dibnah who jumped from his own boat to view it properly.

In 1988 the family moved to France. Peter died there in 2009. Jill (who now has ten grandchildren) and one of her daughters continue to live in France. Her other three children live in England, and Simon still makes a point of driving through Drayton Beauchamp whenever he is in the area. The friendship formed between the Joiner family and the Cook family – the first residents of Beauchamp Barn after its conversion – has survived for over 36 years.

David and Isabel Ogden

In 1984 David and Isabel Ogden bought the Cottage, two families having lived there in the intervening seven years since the Joiners had moved from the village. David's grandfather was a British officer in an Indian Army regiment, but the family returned to England when David's father was a child. David, born in Bournemouth, recalls many moves around England during his own childhood as his father worked as a doctor in the prison service. Isabel was born in Irvine in Scotland but brought up in Prestwick. She trained as a nurse in the Glasgow Western Hospital before coming south to undertake paediatric nursing training at Great Ormond Street, London.

David and Isabel met at St Mary's Hospital, Paddington where they were both working. They lived in London for a short time before spending a few months in Birmingham while waiting to move to Tring. There David took up a position as a General Practitioner. After the birth of their three daughters, Isabel was a full-time homemaker for several years, but returned to work twenty years ago as a teacher, latterly in the prison service. Over the years she also provided the service which was at that time taken for granted as one of the duties of the family doctor's spouse - that of providing from home a contact point for patients with urgent medical needs when David was on call. David retired in 2007 and Isabel in 2008.

The couple were attracted to The Cottage because of its rural location and its quirkiness. With daughters then aged seven, five and almost two, the village was accessible for David's work and for schools in Tring and Berkhamsted. Now, 27 years later, they are about to move away from the village. Because of the lack of a village hall in Drayton Beauchamp, Isabel and David feel that it is harder to arrange casual social gatherings here although they have liked the cross-section of society which one finds in the village. They do not see Drayton Beauchamp as a place in which to grow old, however, and are moving to a larger community where there are more amenities within walking distance. They have also chosen to move to a house which is closer to their children and grandchildren and easier to maintain than The Cottage with its thatched roof which must be replaced every 20 to 25 years, and with a smaller garden.

Old Manor Farm

(formerly Manor Farm or Morgans Farm)

Originally visited in 1911 by an investigator from the Royal Commission on Historical Monuments, Old Manor Farm was described in his report as "a house of two storeys, built in the seventeenth century, restored and enlarged in the eighteenth and nineteenth centuries". In its most recent listing in 1985 under the Town and Country Planning Act of 1971 it is described as: "A Grade II house, seventeenth century or earlier; timber framed and re-fronted in nineteenth century colour washed brick". This substantial house (now with five bedrooms and four public rooms) is thought by its current owners, however, to date back as far as 1490 with additions in 1520 and a dining room added in the early years of Queen Victoria's reign.

In old documents the house is sometimes called Manor Farm and sometimes Morgans - or even Morgan's - Farm. It is not clear where the name "Morgans" originated, but interestingly in 1773 the sum of 19s 6d was paid to the poor from the manor of Drayton by Lucy Manners, the Lady of the Manor from whom the Jenney family inherited the manor and estates of Drayton Beauchamp, and a John Parrott and a Thomas Morgan also paid "as tenants to the parish". In addition, from 1832-1836 Thomas Morgan is listed in the Land Tax Assessment list and other documents as a Churchwarden and the occupier of one of the farms belonging to Lucy Manners.

It is believed that the house would have been built for a yeoman or squire of some standing as the rooms are generously sized and the beams - apart from the very oldest ones which were simply hewn from the felled tree without shaping – are carefully chamfered. There is some thought by the current owners that this house, along with the Dower House, may have been used during the Civil War as a safe house for people escaping from London. Indeed a ghost seen many times by the present owner is dressed in the clothes of that period.

The roof of Old Manor Farm may have been thatched originally, but at some stage a clay tile roof was added. The external walls in some places are of brick, and part of the upper storey is roughcast. In common with the other farmhouses in the village, Old Manor Farm sits sideways to the village lane, with the room which served as a pantry facing away from the sun and therefore cool at all times. The oldest part of the house lies furthest from the lane. A staircase in one corner of the room which was added, the owners believe, in 1520 would have led to the upstairs room used as sleeping quarters by family and visitors together, but this staircase was removed later. Tudor "h" hinges are still in place on some of the original oak doors. In the courtyard at the front of the house are two wells, one of which may have been used as an icehouse.

There are six working fireplaces, three of them uncovered by the present owners, and with chimneys rising up through the centre of the house. The central chimney, original to the house, is of three square shafts with oversailing tops. In one fireplace a child's handmade shoe, believed by the current owners to date back as far as 1520, was discovered tucked carefully into a ledge of the chimney. A bread oven was originally built into the side of one fireplace, but this has been removed, and the little recess which was left would have provided a warm sleeping place for a small baby.

All of the floors have been laid on earth, and grain was found under the floors during renovations. Straw would have been thrown into the house and replaced every week – a practical way of dealing with the sanitation and hygiene problems unavoidable in a house shared by humans and animals alike. Lavender, rosemary and other herbs would have been used to mask the inevitable unpleasant smells.

In the 1838 Tithe Map and accompanying document, Manor and Lower Farms plus 476 acres were owned by William Christopher/Jenney of Drayton Lodge and farmed by John Parrott. He was succeeded as tenant farmer around 1847 by Christopher Williamson whose daughter Maria married into the Jenney family in 1863. In 1855 William Gurney took over Morgans Farm. He was still there in 1871 and carried on the tradition of holding a "harvest home" for his men and their wives in his barn. By 1877 William Gurney had left the farm and John Horwood was tenant farmer. John Horwood, aged 34, is listed as living there in the 1881 Census and in each census and Kelly's Post Office Directory until 1911. He is also named as a village constable, Overseer of the Poor (later called a Guardian) and Parish Clerk for many years. In 1914, deteriorating health forced him to leave farming (his special expertise having been as a breeder of pure Berkshire pigs) and he relinquished the tenancy of Morgans Farm after 37 years although he accepted with pleasure the invitation to attend the Farmers' Dinner in May 1915. In 1918 he died aged 71 in Broughton, near Aylesbury. His name is etched on a beam of the barn which is situated in front of Old Manor Farm – a building which would have been the stable block for the house.

In 1899 there were said to be seven cottages belonging to Morgans Farm - the three "Mansion Cottages" or "Woodbine Cottages" which were combined to form what is now known as the Dower House, the thatched Cottage(s) at the very end of the village nearest to the Lower Icknield Way, and the two cottages (Beauchamp Cottages) which were knocked down and rebuilt in 1955/6. In 1919 the farm plus the seven cottages and more than 235 acres were sold to Leonard Lewin by Stewart William Jenney. Lewin had been interested in the farm as far back as 1914 and seems to have taken over the tenancy that year despite concerns about renovations he believed were needed to the farmhouse and to the cottages "in the meadows" (i.e. the Dower House). Perhaps to appease him, a new Dutch barn (open rather than with four walls) was built in 1914 on the instructions of Stewart William Jenney.

In March 1921 Leonard Lewin sold the estate to Leslie and Charles Webb but only four years later Leslie Webb put Morgans Farm up for sale again. A catalogue produced for the auction on 15th June 1925 lists the estate as comprising the farmhouse and farm buildings (three principal barns and a stable block), the two thatched cottages, the three Mansion Cottages, the two cottages subsequently converted into one house known as Genista, and 235 acres of "very sound pasture and arable land". The two Beauchamp Cottages are not mentioned. It would seem that this auction was unsuccessful, and in early 1926 Leslie Webb gave his son Frederick Power of Attorney for one year to dispose of the estate. He himself emigrated to Windhoek in South West Africa as a farmer, sailing on the Clan MacBean from Liverpool to Walvis Bay, Namibia, on 19th February 1926. A second auction was held on 5th July 1926 to sell the estate, with only one nineteen-acre arable field (Upper Rye Hill) marked on the catalogue as having been already sold. The tenants of the seven cottages remained unchanged apart from the departure during the previous twelve months of one of the three tenants of Mansion Cottages.

Charles Webb died in London in 1927, Leslie Webb (who eventually returned from Namibia and settled in Nottinghamshire) in 1957. Both are buried in the village churchyard.

Between the June 1926 auction and October of that year various transactions seem to have taken place. It would appear that the estate did not sell as a single entity. James Moor Long, a retired bootmaker of Chesham Bois, bought the farmhouse, 62 acres of land, and five cottages (the three Mansion Cottages plus the two Beauchamp Cottages) in July. In October, he bought the two thatched Cottages and 45 further acres of land beyond the crossroads with the Lower Icknield Way towards Puttenham. Immediately, he sold to George MacDonald Brown (one of the founders of the firm of Brown and Merry) Morgans Farm, the two thatched cottages, the three Mansion Cottages and the two Beauchamp Cottages along with 62 acres. (Forty-two of the forty-five acres beyond the Lower Icknield Way were sold by Long to MacDonald Brown in 1928.) It seems likely that the two cottages now known as Genista were sold separately, probably to Harry Dwight of Upper Farm, and possibly in exchange for the two Peartree Cottages. These, like the two Beauchamp Cottages, were sold by George MacDonald Brown's executors to Aylesbury Rural District Council in 1955. In 1927 George MacDonald Brown sold the Dower House and two acres of land to James Alexander Shepherd.

Captain George MacDonald Brown, described in official documents as a Land Agent and with a very active role in the affairs of the Jenney estate as early as 1914, appears to have appointed a manager to run the farm while he and his wife spent much of the time abroad. In 1937 Jim Anns' name first appears on the Electoral Register at Morgans Farm where he worked as a butler, sleeping in a little room above the pantry. During the Second World War, Italian prisoners of war were used as farm workers, hired by the farm manager who lived in The Cottage. George MacDonald Brown died in 1944. His widow remained at Morgans Farm until early 1948, but by June 1948 only two names are listed on the Electoral Register - perhaps caretakers or farm/domestic workers.

In December 1949 Morgans (plus the two thatched Cottages and land extending to 121 acres) were bought by Bill Oliphant who moved to the village with his wife and two daughters, aged around fourteen and nine. In 1968 Bill Oliphant sold the thatched Cottages to Peter Joiner of "The Cottage Men". Bill Oliphant remained at Morgans until 1975 when he converted the large barn which had previously been his dairy into a house for himself and his wife, taking the name "Morgans" with him and renaming the original house Old Manor Farm. The two other large barns belonging to the farm had by 1976 been converted into homes too – the former cattle shed into Dray House and the piggery into Cheyne House.

Andrew and Sandy Strain

In January 1986 Andrew and Sandy Strain bought the house from the family who had lived there for ten years, and moved from Northwick Park to Old Manor Farm with their two children, then aged eighteen months and two years. Sandy is a Cockney born and bred. Andrew was born in Solihull but moved as a child with his parents to Buckinghamshire and latterly to London. The couple had not intended to move to such a small village, but were immediately attracted to the house when they came to visit their friends, the previous owners. Andrew has continued to commute to London where he works as a solicitor. Sandy stopped work as a property developer three years ago. Their children attended schools in Berkhamsted before moving to secondary schools in Aylesbury, catching the Aylesbury school bus at the end of the village lane.

When the Strain family moved in, considerable upgrading was needed to the house's plumbing, electrical system and roof, as well as major work to combat rising damp. Planning permission had already been granted to convert the stable block into a two-bedroomed home, so the family lived there for two years while the main house was being renovated. This stable block is now rented out to tenants. The original block cobble floor was re-laid downstairs and the upstairs windows were restored so as to keep to the shape of the original doors out of which the sacks of grain would have been thrown.

Sandy describes the house as a "living entity" which does not take kindly to major changes and which would be ruined by attempts to "modernise" it. At the same time, it requires a great deal of ongoing maintenance to preserve its character and its beauty.

The family have no current plans to move, but note with some regret that the village now seems to consist of "houses along a road" rather than constituting a true community. There is no neutral meeting place and there are few events open to all. For those who are new to the village or unfamiliar with many of the residents, the idea of a Parish Meeting held in a private home can feel daunting, and attendance at events held in the church can be equally daunting for those who do not belong to the Church of England. On the other hand, greater use of the church as a community resource for purely social events might serve to bring villagers together and increase a sense of community spirit and involvement.

MORGANS

Chris & Alistair Dunbar & Family

THE DRAY HOUSE

Erica Godman's Pony Express

CHEYNE HOUSE

Anthony & Elizabeth Dutton

Morgans

Morgans, which sits at right angles to the village lane and beyond the building now known as Old Manor Farm, was originally the dairy and cattle shed for the farm. With an external cladding of elm and a clay tile roof, this large building is heavily timbered internally. "Built 1820" is deeply cut into one of its beams.

In 1975 Bill and Barbara Oliphant sold Morgans/Manor Farm and moved to this barn which they had newly commissioned to be converted into a dwelling, taking the name "Morgans" with them to their new home and renaming the former Morgans Farm "Old Manor Farm".

Even in extreme old age Bill Oliphant continued to take an active interest in property and land in Drayton Beauchamp, and to enjoy the beauty of his garden, particularly the fish ponds which he had had dug out around 1959 and which for some time were run as a Trout Farm. These ponds are fed by a stream which ends up in Wilstone Reservoir. Barbara Oliphant died in 1989 and Bill Oliphant in 1995, aged 92. Both are buried in Wilstone Churchyard.

Alistair and Chris Dunbar

Later in 1995, Alistair and Chris Dunbar bought Morgans from the Oliphants' daughters, moving there from Aston Clinton with their own daughter, aged six, and their son, aged four. Alistair, an actuary, was brought up in Harrogate while Chris, an IT manager, originates from Bierton near Aylesbury. The two met at work in Aylesbury and lived in Aylesbury after marrying before moving to Aston Clinton. Morgans was exactly what they had been looking for – the "right house at the right time" - a large property in a village with extensive gardens and several ponds and with opportunities for gardening, bird watching and other country and conservation pursuits. They were delighted to have found a house which had retained such a large garden – eight-and-a-half acres in all - rather than one with a small garden and extensive paddocks.

Although living in Drayton Beauchamp meant that Alistair and Chris had to spend considerable time for several years driving their children to and from junior school near Princes Risborough and to the various after-school activities in which they were involved, the family as a whole felt that the benefits of life at Morgans outweighed any inconveniences. Both children attended grammar schools in Aylesbury and are now at university.

Morgans continues to present the couple with the challenges and projects they relish. The house itself has five bedrooms and four public rooms - one a dining room with a gallery and vaulted ceiling. The major internal change they have made has been to extend widthwise the long, narrow kitchen. This made necessary the repitching and slating of part of the roof. Outside, the couple have gardened enthusiastically, have dug a further large pond for ducks, and have brought in chickens, geese, ducks and fish.

Interestingly, an area of grassland which now forms part of the rear of their estate and that of The Dray House and Cheyne House is called "Ghost Field" or "Ghost Close" on old maps. An expert in Buckinghamshire field names believes that this field is so named because its flat and rather boggy location would have caused will o' the wisps to appear at dusk, without doubt a frightening sight for superstitious villagers of the past.

Adding to the many ghost stories told in the village, Chris reports that she has noticed on several occasions the smell of cigar smoke in the barn in their garden, and when they were new residents the eerie experience of regularly finding the inhalers used by their daughter inexplicably empty. Bill Oliphant was not only asthmatic but also a cigar smoker....

Alistair and Chris like the village which they see as different to other, more conventional villages in that it is very small, self-contained, unspoilt, and rural but not far from London, airports and most facilities. Neighbours were friendly and welcoming when they moved into the village just before Christmas 1995, and the couple continue to enjoy the balance between friendliness and privacy. They have no wish for major changes to be made to the village in which they feel proud to live, and believe that development and the provision of additional amenities could prove to be more damaging than helpful. Chris and Alistair do not envisage that they will move elsewhere.

The Dray House

The Dray House is a large timber building which was originally a hay barn belonging to Manor/Morgans Farm. It was bought from Bill Oliphant in 1973 by Robert Kennedy Ping who, along with John Parker, converted it into a four-bedroomed house. One of the painters who worked on the barn during its conversion was Phil Kempster, husband of Betty Kempster who was born in 1936 in The Cottage at the bottom end of the village. The Dray House was subsequently sold in 1976 to Karl Heinz Hormel, then in October 1979 to Dave Lee Travis, and finally in 1985 to Mike and Erica Godman.

Initially, the newly-named Morgans, Cheyne House and The Dray House each had a field of half-an-acre, but eventually these fields passed to The Dray House, giving it its current size of just over two acres which includes the driveway and the land on which the house sits. No changes have been made to the shape of The Dray House itself since its original conversion apart from the addition of a conservatory in 2003.

Mike and Erica Godman

Mike originated from Hampshire and his great-grandfather has gone down in history as the man who built the chimes of Big Ben. Erica was born at Shardeloes near Amersham of English and Czechoslovakian parentage. In 1985 when Mike and Erica moved from Bovingdon to Drayton Beauchamp their four children ranged in age from eighteen down to three years. Mike's career was in computing; Erica taught periodically and developed an enthusiastic and time-absorbing interest in wildlife. Mike died in 2001 and Erica has remained in The Dray House, sharing the house and grounds with – currently – two ponies, six snakes, two cats, twelve tortoises, three pipistrelle bats and three stick insects. She is Bat Warden for the village, works as a volunteer at Whipsnade Zoo and with several other organisations, and is a familiar sight around the village lanes with her trap pulled by one or two ponies. An annual feature of Christmas in Drayton Beauchamp is Erica's "Pony Express" – the delivery of Christmas cards for the residents of Drayton Beauchamp and Buckland by pony and trap, a unique venture which Erica carries out for fun but which also raises money for charity.

Erica recounts stories about amusing events in this unusual village. Among these is the story told by a former farm worker who recalled shooting with an air rifle at rats from one of the high crossbeams in what is now her reception room while he sat up there eating his lunchtime sandwich. There was also a noted occasion when bats gained entry through the weatherboards into Cheyne House and triggered the burglar alarm. Other highlights were the rescue from Erica's snow-covered swimming pool of the Shetland pony which had fallen in, and soon afterwards the lengthy attempt to capture a neighbour's ornamental duck which had also arrived in the swimming pool and seemed reluctant to leave.

Erica notes, as have others, the lack of a public meeting-place in the village apart from the church which may not, for non-churchgoers, seem an appropriate social centre. This lack may make it more difficult for newcomers to become known to, and accepted by, established residents. On the other hand, she acknowledges that the village is probably too small to sustain another public building and wonders if some events could be arranged jointly with Buckland which has a well-used village hall. Periodically she contemplates the idea of moving to a smaller house now that her children are grown up and living away from home, but she is very happy here and could not bear to leave either The Dray House or Drayton Beauchamp.

Cheyne House

This elm-clad dwelling was originally the tractor and farm equipment shed for the nearby Old Manor Farm (formerly Morgans Farm). An inscription chiselled into a beam gives the date "1872", but a farm building on the same site (although at right angles to the lane) shows up clearly on a map of the village dated 1736. On the Ordnance Survey map of 1877, the barn room of Cheyne House is definitely in its current position, but with an area of water immediately between it and the village lane.

On 8th October, 1973 this barn was sold by William Oliphant to John Michael Parker of Beaconsfield. It seems that it was bought simply so that it could be converted and then sold, and no residents are registered as living there until Denis and Sarah Boyle purchased Cheyne House in 1977.

The tractor barn, sitting lengthwise to the village lane, was originally open at the rear but this space was glassed in, and a sizeable extension then added at right angles. After purchasing Cheyne House, the Boyles dug up old timbers from a collapsed stable block discovered behind the barn and incorporated these into a raised and "fenced" section of the main barn room. Cheyne House now consists of four bedrooms, two main reception rooms, a "cinema", office and annexe, and sits in grounds of almost an acre.

Anthony and Elizabeth Dutton

In April 1998 Cheyne House was sold by Sarah Boyle, by then widowed, to Anthony and Elizabeth Dutton, the present owners, who took up residence together with Elizabeth's ten-year old daughter Alexa in August of that year.

Both Anthony and Elizabeth Dutton have led much more adventurous and well-travelled lives than the villagers of Drayton Beauchamp a century ago would have dreamt possible. Anthony originates from Gloucestershire where his father worked as a Local Authority accountant before and after service with the RAF during World War II. Anthony himself worked firstly as a management trainee, and then for a year as a young man in Buenos Aires teaching in his uncle's Anglo-Argentinean school before setting off with two friends to ride on horseback the 1200 miles to Bolivia, a journey which would take several months. Back in Argentina, he stayed for a while on a farm owned by a man called Leach, one of whose ancestors, by amazing coincidence, had originally settled there from Ivinghoe in the early nineteenth century. After his return to England (where he arrived on the day that John Kennedy was killed) Anthony worked in the travel industry and then as a director of Gabbitas Thring Services, an educational consultancy. Finally he took up work in the film industry, first as a sound recordist and then as a cameraman. In this role, he twice joined Sir Ranulph Fiennes' expedition to the South Pole in December 1979. He also trained as a pilot and in 1984/5 built with some assistance his own single-seater plane in which he hoped to fly round the world from Pole to Pole. This plan, sadly, had to be abandoned because of lack of sponsorship, but not before Anthony and his plane had appeared in the Blue Peter studios where he was interviewed by Janet Ellis. Subsequently Anthony has ridden his motorbike to the north of Norway beyond the Arctic Circle, to Bosnia, and to other far-flung destinations. He retired from work ten years ago.

Elizabeth was brought up in Cambridge and Newmarket where her father was a Consultant Pathologist. In 1965 after secretarial training she found work as a nanny in California, moving on from this to make programmes and write scripts for a classical music radio station in San Francisco. She then went to South America where she financed her travels by writing articles for a Miami-based travel magazine. After returning to England she spent two years at the National Sound Archive with part responsibility for the oral history collection before completing a degree in Development Studies at the University of East Anglia and undertaking postgraduate work at the University of Leicester. More recently she added a teaching certificate to her other qualifications. Elizabeth has also spent time in Kenya, Zambia and Zimbabwe where she worked for UNESCO. She has been employed, too, as a consultant for a small firm specialising in support for workers' co-operatives. Currently she is a self-employed consultant researcher working part-time to evaluate projects connected with inner city regeneration.

Anthony, who has two daughters and two grandchildren, and Elizabeth, who has one daughter, met through a common friend in 1993 and married in 1996. Anthony had lived in Amersham since 1975 but was keen to move to a house with more space for the film equipment he rented out. At the same time, he needed to be located within easy reach of the BBC at White City and Shepherd's Bush. He discovered Drayton Beauchamp by chance while riding his motorbike through the village. Elizabeth, a committed city dweller, was less keen to move to such a tiny village but was won over by the fact that Drayton Beauchamp seemed not picture postcard perfect, but was instead a "proper" village with a lovely church and an eclectic mix of residents.

The couple have never regretted coming to the village, describing it as welcoming, happy and neighbourly, with a strong feeling of community spirit. Since moving in, they have carried out only minor internal changes to Cheyne House and have no plans for further structural changes. They have no plans, either, to move away, and would like to stay for as long as they remain physically able to manage a large house and not to feel defeated by the distance of the village from amenities. For the moment, they try to satisfy the restless streak to which they both admit by continuing to travel, and indeed they returned to Argentina for visits in 2008 and 2010. When asked about changes to the village which they believe might improve the amenities or quality of life here, Anthony described an "ideal world" where there would be a meeting place of some sort in the village – perhaps a village green with a pub or hall. He recognises, however, that it would be immensely difficult in practical terms to create such a facility and to deal with the additional traffic and noise to which it would give rise.

The Dower House

The Dower House is believed to date from around 1620 and is likely to have been built by a wealthy husband for use as his widow's residence after his death, a practice which released the principal manor for the new heir. In this case, it would almost certainly have been the Dower House to the local Drayton Beauchamp manor, held by the Cheyne family from 1364 until the death of William Cheyne, Viscount Newhaven, in 1728. It is believed that the house was the dower of a Mary Cheyne, who lived there for only a few years after her husband's death until she too died. In 1603 Queen Elizabeth I granted to Francis Cheyne and Mary his wife, "their heirs and assigns for ever", the manor of Drayton Beauchamp. They were certainly living in the village in 1612 when the trial was held of a man accused of stealing sheep from Francis. Francis was buried on 12th January 1619 aged 72 and Mary on 25th February 1629 and both are believed to be buried beneath the chancel in the village church. In Francis's Will, drawn up shortly before his death, he specifies that he wishes to be buried in the chancel of the parish church of Drayton Beauchamp "where many of my worthy ancestors before me are interred". He also states his wish that his wife should remain in the house in Drayton Beauchamp "where we have long inhabited together". Although by this he seems to have been envisaging that his wife would remain in the manor house which then stood close by the church, sharing it with his heir, it may be that the heir - his nephew Francis whom he appointed as his executor - did not like this proposed living arrangement and instead had the The Dower House built for his widowed aunt.

Research is still needed to establish what happened to The Dower House in the two centuries between the death of its first owner and 1838 when the Tithe Map was drawn up. It is certainly clearly depicted on the beautiful "Mapp of the Mannour of Drayton Beauchamp" dated 1736.

In 1838 the Tithe Map and Apportionment Document list The Dower House as part of the estate of William Christopher/Jenney of Drayton Lodge, and lived in by three separate tenant families. It is thought that in the nineteenth century the three cottages – sometimes called Mansion Cottages, Woodbine Cottages, Town Houses, Drayton Meadow or even "In the Meadows" - were lived in rent-free by the poorest of the villagers. Indeed in the 1871 Census one cottage was tenanted by a "pauper on the parish", the second by a widow, and the third by a man "unable to see". For many years the three cottages were used to house agricultural workers at Morgans Farm and a box of old shoes found in recent years in the house is believed to date back to those days.

In 1927, however, the three cottages (of which only two were by then occupied) - along with two acres - were sold by George MacDonald Brown (owner of Morgans Farm since October 1926) to James Alexander Shepherd of St Leonards, a stockbroker in London, who had them converted back from three "one-up, one-down" cottages into a single dwelling which he used as a weekend cottage. The Dower House featured in "Ideal Home" around 1947.

In October 1985 The Dower House was given a Grade II listing under the Town and Country Planning Act of 1971. It was inspected again in 2004, five years after English Heritage assumed responsibility for documenting the records of English historical monuments, and its grading status was confirmed. It is described in its listing as a building which "followed the vernacular tradition but was sufficiently advanced to have a symmetrical entrance front". This main entrance is actually on the north side of the house facing away from the village lane and with traces remaining of the old carriage drive which led around to it. The front door opens on to a "baffle entry" with the main chimneybreast immediately ahead in the centre of the house. A passage leads left to the sitting room and right to what would have been the "hall" or main day–to-day living room of the house. In this room is the principal fireplace, complete with bread oven and the holes into which the hooks for suspending cooking pots would have been inserted.

Construction of the house is of timber frame with brick infill - an early and well-preserved example of its kind. Ceilings are high and the steeply pitched roof is thatched. The original building is thought to have been extended around 1700 when an additional service room cum pantry was built with a single storey lean-to adjoining. At the other end of the house was a lean-to cart shed. A track leading past the side of the house is thought to have joined up with the road to Wilstone in the days before the creation of the reservoirs at the beginning of the 19th century made necessary the diversion of local tracks and roads.

Old maps of the village show The Dower House with a V-shaped pond on the left of the track leading from the house to the village lane, and with at least four cottages along this track. A chapter entitled "Memories of Drayton Beauchamp" in the book "Sketches of the Buckinghamshire Countryside" written by Horace Harman in 1934 describes at length an Ann Wright (1800-1873) who lived in one of these cottages with her mother. A fuller account of Ann Wright ("old Annie the herbalist") appears in the chapter about Beauchamp Cottages. Ann's cottage and the others along The Dower House driveway were eventually demolished. Old maps also show how much water there was in the village in the shape of streams and ponds. Indeed there was a ford at the end of The Dower House driveway and the stream crossed the lane through a culvert nearby. A toddler is said to have drowned in this culvert in the 1940s, but extensive research has so far found no official record of this.

Two embalmed cats were discovered several years ago in the loft of The Dower House (placed there to ensure good fortune or to ward off evil forces, perhaps), and many fragments of blue and white china buried in the garden. In the 1950s a musket powder container was found by the side of the stream and the present owners have found old marbles under a floor, a silver and enamel Art Deco brooch in the garden, and a beautiful green glass dice. Former owners of Cheyne House nearby dug up cannonballs in their garden some years ago. The previous owners of The Dower House were convinced that it was haunted, telling of seeing ghostly figures in the garden and Roundhead soldiers inside the house. The current owners have experienced none of these.

One notable previous owner of The Dower House was Alfred Reynolds (1884-1969), conductor and composer of light music, who studied under Max Bruch before World War I. Alfred Reynolds lived at The Dower House with his sister Edith from 1945 or perhaps some years earlier (no Electoral Registers were produced from 1940-45) until 1959, composing most of his music on a grand piano in the sitting room of The Dower House. He hosted village events (for instance a fête to celebrate the 1953 Coronation), and the house was frequently visited by well-known figures from the world of music and the arts (A A Milne, for example). Alfred's niece came to stay with him during the war, working as a Land Girl at Morgans Farm and marrying in the village church in 1945. She continued to live there for several years with her son, born in 1947, while her husband was in the Submarine Service. The family told the present owners about a whirlwind which swept across the fields behind The Dower House while they were living there, narrowly missing the house. (This may well be the same tornado which other former villagers have described as having lifted off the roof of a barn at Upper Farm as it passed through the village in 1950.) The Reynolds moved to Bognor Regis in 1959 and Alfred died there ten years later.

The connection with the arts continued with the next owners, the two Misses Dewick, who are believed to have been connected to the Liberty family and to have been the aunts of the actor Nigel Havers. The sisters retired to the village after selling their school which stood on the site of what is now Brent Cross. They lived in The Dower House for almost thirty years, dying within three months of each other in late 1990/early 1991.

Stuart and Julie Wilson

Julie and Stuart Wilson bought The Dower House in 1993 from a couple who had lived there for only two years. Julie, who originates from County Down in Northern Ireland, and Stuart, from County Durham, met at Manchester Art College. They lived firstly in London, and then in several villages near Drayton Beauchamp before moving in December 1993 to The Dower House, attracted to the seclusion of the house with its excellent views, its extensive grounds of almost three acres, and its proximity to the nearby nature reserves. Their children were ten and eight at the time, but both are now living independently away from home. Julie is by profession a textile designer, while Stuart writes and films commercials in this country and abroad. The Dower House itself has been used as a film location several times.

The couple thought briefly in 2004 of moving to Scotland, but have now decided that they are very happy where they are and have abandoned all plans to move away. They do not mind the geographical separation of The Dower House from the village and feel that they are living in the perfect location where they can enjoy their garden, the abundant wildlife around them, and the rare pheasants which Stuart breeds and rears. Their one suggestion for improving the village is that it would be good if there were a focal point such as a pub or shop.

THE DOWER HOUSE

Stuart & Julie Wilson

Esmé & Alan Southam & Family 1972

DRAYTON COTTAGE c.1972

GENISTA

Martin & Fiona Green

Ruth Akerman (née Ball)

Ruth, almost 92 but still working until only four years ago, was born in one of the four cottages which used to stand in the lane leading to the Dower House, and was the only child of Clare and Arthur Ball. Members of the Ball family were resident in Drayton Beauchamp at least as far back as the beginning of the nineteenth century, with members of their extended family in nearby Buckland and Wilstone.

In the 1891 Census Ruth's father is recorded as the four-year-old son of Walter and Elizabeth Ball and with older brothers Harry, thirteen, Ernest, ten, and Edgar, seven. By the 1901 Census he was working as a fourteen-year-old carter, and now also had three younger siblings - Nellie, nine, Herbert, three, and Daisy, eleven months. The family were living at Lower Farm and Arthur's father Walter was farm bailiff to the Jenney family. Ruth remembers her father describing how he used to milk cows at six a.m. in the cowshed. This was later used for pigs, and was finally converted in the 1970s into Long Barn.

Although Ruth no longer lives in the village she retains strong connections with it. Both of her parents are buried in the churchyard, and her cousin Michael Anns lives at 2 Peartree Cottages (Michael being the grandson of Edgar Ball and his wife Amy and the nephew of Ruth's father Arthur). Ruth's cousin Reg Price (son of Nellie, Arthur's younger sister), now almost ninety-five, lives with his wife Lorna in nearby Aston Clinton. Other cousins Richard Gregory and Richard's sister Margaret Dean (also grandchildren of Edgar and Amy Ball) live within a few miles of the village and retain close links with it too.

Ruth has lived in Drayton Beauchamp on three separate occasions. Born in the village, she moved with her family to Northchurch when she was three, then to Halton two years later. She returned to Drayton Beauchamp in 1930, living with her parents in one of the two cottages which together are now called Badgers End (then known as Ballad Cottages) but she left as a young adult to join the Land Army. Her parents meanwhile moved to the White House on the canal at Bucklandwharf, but returned to Drayton Beauchamp around 1938 to live at Peartree Cottages. Ruth herself also came back just before she married in 1944 and is listed on the Electoral Register for several years along with her parents. Ruth's husband, in the meantime, was serving in Egypt as a soldier. Her first son was eighteen months old before his father was demobilised.

Ruth's father was verger at St Mary's Church for a number of years during the incumbency of the Reverend D J Scurry Jones as Rector. After the Second World War Drayton Beauchamp, in common with other Buckinghamshire parishes, collected donations to be given to returning servicemen and women. This ceremony took place in the village schoolroom and the Reverend Scurry Jones made the presentation. The schoolroom was also used for services for a time when repairs to the church were being carried out. Ruth remembers that church attendance was in those days a regular commitment for many people, with the local church attracting its congregation from as far away as Tring. She recalls a Tring man, Bert Nutkins, coming from Tring to St Mary's. He was uncle to Phyllis (née Nutkins) and Vic Humphreys who lived in the village in the late 1930s. Another Nutkins – Frederick James – lived in the village from 1927-30 and was nicknamed "Duckie" because of his frequent use of this affectionate greeting. It may have been Fred's wife Lilian who ran the village shop from her front room at Ballad Cottages, outside which were the village pump and well. When Ruth and her parents moved to this cottage there were hopes that her mother would keep the shop going, but Clare declined.

Ruth recalls three ways of leaving the village - across the fields to the bus stop at Bucklandwharf, up the Holloway to the Upper Icknield Way with its bus service to Tring and Aylesbury, or down to the crossroads on the Lower Icknield Way where a bus stopped twice a week. Each option involved a fair walk before public transport could be reached, but at a time when few parish residents had their own car this was considered completely acceptable, even by young children.

Ruth pictures the Drayton Beauchamp of her childhood as a farming village populated mainly by farming people – Rye Hill Farm, Church Hill Farm, Bridge Farm, Upper Farm, Lower Farm, Morgans Farm and Rectory Farm (the smallholding between the Rectory and the Schoolhouse). Local men were mostly employed on the farms, starting work at a young age. She recalls clearly many of the village families of the time – for instance the Balls, Catos, Ballads, Kempsters and Howletts. For Ruth, the feeling that there were close bonds of affection and readily-available mutual assistance between villagers was particularly strong given that she herself was part of such a large family whose roots were deeply established in the Drayton Beauchamp soil.

Garth and Betty Beckett

Born in London, Betty Beckett survived the Blitz as a small child - taking refuge in the Underground Stations at night along with so many other Londoners - and was evacuated three times (to Essex, Wimbledon and finally the Cotswolds). After being demobilised from the Army at the end of the war her father was eventually appointed as a security guard for the Rothschilds at Waddesdon Manor and Betty moved into a flat above the stables with her family. Her future husband Garth Beckett was born and brought up in Upper Winchendon and carried out his National Service in Cyprus. Betty and Garth met at a village dance in Waddesdon, and in 1954 the couple came as newly-weds to live in Drayton Beauchamp, not far from Garth's sister and her family who had Moat Farm in Wilstone.

They lived first of all in Devereux, one of the two cottages (now known as 1 Beauchamp Cottages) which had been owned by Captain George MacDonald Brown of Morgans Farm but which after his death in 1944 were rented out partly-furnished for £1 5s per week by Brown and Merry. Devereux (probably named after tenants of the 1940s Thomas and Mary Devereux) was the cottage nearer to the lane leading to the Dower House. Brick-built and with a slate roof, it had a red and black quarry-tile floor in the kitchen and living room, stairs leading up to the bedrooms from the kitchen, and a large old fireplace in the living room. Altogether it seemed to the young Becketts that this cottage, situated in a village which appeared to be "stuck in a time warp", was the most romantic and the prettiest setting imaginable in which to begin married life. In reality, the Devereux drains had collapsed, there was only one tap in the butler's sink in the kitchen, the log fire smoked, and the privy was in the back garden. Even worse, the water would freeze in the bungalow bath when Betty soaked nappies in it during the cold winter days of 1955 after her daughter's birth, and she was reduced to trying to break the ice with a pickaxe. Despite this, the couple considered that the charm of this two-up, two-down cottage more than compensated for the disadvantages. The stream ran alongside their home parallel to the lane leading to the Dower House, and the garden and fields behind the cottage provided an ideal world in which children could explore and play. Their next-door neighbours in the cottage adjoining Devereux were Amy and Edgar Ball, Mick Anns' maternal grandparents. The Balls' cottage was still known in the 1950s as the less romantic "2 Morgans Farm Cottages".

In February 1955 the two cottages were deemed "unfit for human habitation" and in July of that year were sold to Aylesbury Rural District Council (along with the two Peartree Cottages) for £100 altogether. Anxious to demolish and rebuild the two Morgans Farm Cottages, ARDC urged the Becketts to move to one of the Upper Farm Cottages owned by the farmer Harry Nicholls, with the promise that this would help to speed their progress towards the top of the waiting list for Council accommodation in Aston Clinton. Their daughter was born in December 1955 and was around a year old when they moved from Devereux to 1 Upper Farm Cottages (the cottage farther from the farm) with Maureen and Michael

Hannon as their neighbours in number 2. There was still the disadvantage of an outside privy but, as at Devereux, the incomparable uninterrupted views behind the house towards the reservoir. (After the Becketts left this cottage, it and the cottage next door were converted into one house by Michael Hannon, a builder by trade. In 1977 this house, now named Genista, was sold by Gordon Nicholls to Paul and Jean Welford.)

Betty and Garth lived in 1 Upper Farm Cottages for three years before being offered a move to 1 Peartree Cottages, which had been newly modernised and where Garth laid a driveway which Betty notes with interest is still in use sixty years later. By coincidence, their neighbours at number 2 were (until he died in 1962) Edgar Ball, who had been their neighbour along with his wife Amy when they lived at Devereux, and Jim and Marjorie Anns, Edgar's daughter and son-in-law.

The Council offered to sell the Becketts 1 Peartree Cottages for £1500 but this seemed a poor bargain given that at that time a house could be bought on the newly-built Bedgrove estate for only £500 more. In any case, 1 Peartree Cottages had only two bedrooms and the Becketts by now had two children, their son having been born in 1962 in the upstairs bedroom of their cottage. Accordingly, in 1964 they moved to Tring Road in Aylesbury, bringing to an end their ten-year stay in Drayton Beauchamp.

Looking back at their years in the village, Betty remembers social gatherings at the old schoolhouse which was at that time used as a village meeting-place, and especially the greatly enjoyed monthly visit by the mobile library which stopped in the lane outside the schoolhouse. In an era when most villagers had no access to a car and catching a bus meant a lengthy walk to the top of the Holloway or down to the crossroads on the Lower Icknield Way, many local businesses ran vans which made frequent visits to the village. Betty remembers Gower's of Tring selling hardware of all kinds in this way, Gregory's of Long Marston selling butcher meat, Howlett's selling bakery items, the Co-operative and International Stores selling groceries. A laundry van also made regular trips to the village to collect and deliver the heavy items like sheets which could not be laundered in the tiny cottages.

Betty remembers too the regular bicycle rides with her small daughter sitting in a seat behind her as they travelled to and from the primary school in Aston Clinton. Eventually Betty learned to drive and was allowed to park her car in the farmyard at Upper Farm, where her parking manoeuvres caused Harry Nicholls endless amusement. When the Becketts came to the village, Florrie, Edie and Fred Ballad were still at Lower Farm. Betty does not recall ever meeting Fred who died in 1957 but she clearly remembers a major sale of goods at Lower Farm before the two elderly sisters moved from there to The Homestead soon after Fred's death.

The Becketts' son was still very young when they left the village, but Betty remembers with pleasure the happiness of her daughter's childhood years there. The reservoir and the moats in the field opposite Upper Farm were favourite places for children (among them her own little girl, plus Margaret Gregory, the Hannons' two daughters, and the daughter and twin sons of the Walls who lived at The Close) to play and have picnics. Unfettered by the anxieties of 21st century parents, and secure in an area where they knew – and were known by – everyone, the village children of that era were able to explore their environment together and to develop qualities of self-reliance and commonsense.

Sadly, Garth died in 1988. The couple's daughter now lives in Oxford and their son in Bristol but Betty herself still lives within a very few miles of Drayton Beauchamp and retains great affection for the village.

Beauchamp Cottages

Two cottages stood on the site of the present-day 1 and 2 Beauchamp Cottages 175 years ago and perhaps even earlier. In the 1838 Tithe Map and accompanying Apportionment Document, the two cottages are listed as being owned by William Christopher/Jenney. The tenants of these two cottages in 1838 were James Kipping and Elias Watley. Indeed, church baptismal records confirm that Elias and Hannah Watley were living in the village as early as 1813 although the exact address is not given. It is almost certain that Elias Watley is the same man as the "Elias Wortley" mentioned on the Cottesloe Hundreds Militia Ballot List of 1812 as living in the village and being given exemption from having to serve in the militia on the grounds of "scald head, appealed twice and discharged". James Kipping and his wife Sophia and Elias along with Hannah Watley are again listed at these cottages in the 1841 Census. Hannah Watley died in 1856, Elias in 1860, Sophia Kipping in 1870 and James in 1872.

Lodging with the Watleys in 1841 were Jane Wright and her daughter Hannah (or Ann). Immortalised in Horace Harman's "Sketches of the Buckinghamshire Countryside" (1934), Ann Wright - born in Drayton Beauchamp in 1801 - was a poor straw plaiter who, along with her mother, had lived in one of the now-demolished cottages near the village pond which lay beside what is nowadays the driveway to the Dower House. Abject poverty seems to have driven the two women to give up their cottage and to take lodgings with the Watleys. Jane died in February 1851, and in the census of that year Ann was still lodging with the Watleys, but now sharing her cramped accommodation with Harriet Smith (10), one of a series of protégées to whom she taught the art of straw plaiting. Until she died in 1873 "Old Ann" seems to have held a special place in her fellow villagers' affections - loved and respected by adults and children alike, and often consulted for her country lore and her potent herbal remedies.

In the 1861 Census John Hedges, aged fifteen and born in Wilstone, is listed as living in the village with George and Ann Ball to whom he was related. John married in 1874 and took on the tenancy of one of these cottages, living there with his wife Sarah (née Lovegrove, sister of John Lovegrove the Jenney estate's gamekeeper who lived at Fiddlers Green). They had five children, the eldest of whom died in infancy. Their youngest son Frank John, born in 1892, emigrated to Canada in 1912 intending to become a farmer there. Frank was married in July 1915 to a young woman of Scottish origin and only five days later he enlisted as a Private in the Canadian Overseas 1st Battalion. He was killed in action in April 1917 at Vimy Ridge four days before the main Canadian offensive. His name appears on the commemorative mural tablet in the village church and a haunting photograph of him as a small boy is reproduced in this book.

Walter, the youngest child of John and Sarah Hedges, lived his entire life in the village until his death in 1965 and was for many years sexton of the village church. Walter ("Tom") and his wife Charlotte ("Lottie") had nine children. One daughter died as a baby and a son Frank James who was almost certainly named after his uncle Frank is recorded in the village church Burial Register as having died on 22nd May 1926 aged seven. It seems that poor Frank died of the injuries he sustained as a result of being knocked down by a motorcycle and sidecar near Drayton Lodge. An inquest was held and a verdict of accidental death was reached. The couple's third child, Dorothy Primrose but always known locally as Peggy, lived almost all of her long life in Drayton Beauchamp. Peggy served with the Women's Royal Naval Service and moved away for a short time with her husband Charlie to Aston Clinton before returning to the village and to the house which is now 1 Beauchamp Cottages.

The two cottages traditionally housed workers employed at Morgans Farm. In 1944 the then owner of Morgans Farm, George MacDonald Brown, died. In 1949 Morgans Farm was sold to William Oliphant, but neither of these two cottages was included in this sale and both seem to have continued to be rented out by Brown and Merry, the firm which George MacDonald Brown had helped to found. In 1955 both cottages and the two Peartree Cottages were sold for a total of £100 to Aylesbury Rural District Council by the National Provincial Bank, executor for George MacDonald Brown. The two Beauchamp Cottages had been deemed unfit for human habitation in October 1954, and both were now demolished. In place of the two-up-one-down cottages, two bungalows were erected by James Chandler & Sons of Long Marston, building contractors to the Council in the 1950s.

1 Beauchamp Cottages

The final tenants at number 1 (by this stage called Devereux) before the cottages were demolished were Betty and Garth Beckett who then moved to one of the Upper Farm Cottages (now Genista). Their village experiences are described elsewhere.

Tom and Lottie Hedges, who had lived for several years across the lane in one of the Lower Farm Cottages (now Setherwood), crossed back over the lane in 1957 to the newly-rebuilt 1 Beauchamp Cottages. They were joined by their daughter Peggy who retained the tenancy of the cottage after Tom died in 1965 and Lottie in 1970. In 1990 Aylesbury Vale District Council sold the cottage to Peggy who subsequently sold it to Bob Shuttle, staying on as his tenant until she died in 1994. In 1999 1 Beauchamp Cottages was sold to Jane Allam who extended it in 2004. The cottage now has a spacious hall, living room, two large bedrooms (both en-suite) and a family kitchen and bathroom.

Tim Hill and Ashley McLure

Since 2007 Tim Hill and Ashley McLure have rented this bungalow from Jane Allam. Ashley spent her first eleven years in Zambia and Sierra Leone before moving back to the United Kingdom with her family and settling with them in Northamptonshire. When she met Tim she was working as a P A at Thame Farmers' Market whilst he had film construction and antiques businesses and was living in Waddesdon. The two found 1 Beauchamp Cottages on an Internet property site and were immediately attracted to it when they visited. Their son was born in November 2009 and although they still like the cottage and its rural setting immensely, they now feel the need for a rather larger home. They would like to stay in this area which is convenient for Tim's work running his business and they would not want to live in a more urban setting. Ashley has a good circle of friends - many, like herself, mothers with young children - within a few miles of Drayton Beauchamp, and she has found those villagers she has met to be welcoming and friendly. She is alarmed by the speed of traffic coming through the pavement-less village when she is out walking with her little boy in his buggy, but the disadvantage of having to use a car for most journeys is, she feels, more than compensated for by being able to live in one of the few quiet backwaters left in this part of the country.

130

BATES BOATYARD

THE STABLES   Debbie La-Haye & Dave Johnson & Family

1 & 2 BEAUCHAMP COTTAGES

2 Beauchamp Cottages

The final tenants of what had been the old 2 Morgans Cottages and the first tenants of what were now the new 2 Beauchamp Cottages were Amy and Edgar Ball, Mick Anns' grandparents, and their son Billy. Billy died in 1952 and Amy in 1958. In 1959 Edgar moved to 2 Peartree Cottages, the home of his daughter Margery, where he died in 1961. Two sets of tenants followed Edgar at 2 Beauchamp Cottages – one for twenty years and one for twelve.

Allan and Lilian Jacques

The present tenants of 2 Beauchamp Cottages are Allan and Lilian Jacques. Allan was born in Keswick where his mother was a school teacher. When he was still a young boy, his family moved to Kent where his father took over a farm and ran it very successfully. During World War II Allan served with the Royal Naval Air Service, the Fleet Air Arm, and served on both HMS Illustrious and HMS Formidable. He then worked for the Atomic Energy Establishment for many years, based in Dorset but travelling countrywide in connection with his work.

Lilian was born in Highgate but moved to Middlesex when she was ten. After marrying, she and her first husband lived in Essex before moving to Aylesbury. Her husband then died, leaving her with two sons to bring up. Allan (by this stage divorced and with three daughters) and Lilian met on a coach when both were – completely independently – travelling to Falmouth on holiday. They married in 1975 and lived first in Weymouth and then in Aylesbury. In 1991 they moved to 2 Beauchamp Cottages.

Both Allan and Lilian have suffered some health problems, so 2 Beauchamp Cottages is ideal for their needs with its two public rooms, one bedroom, a kitchen and bathroom, all on one level. Their car makes it possible for them to drive easily to shops and to wherever else they want to go. They find the cottage warm and comfortable, love the open rural views at the rear, and feel happy and settled in the village. They enjoy crosswords and reading and do not find time hanging heavily. They feel sad that they are no longer able to maintain the garden as they used to, but family members help when they can. The one change they would like to see in the village is the provision of mains drainage.

Drayton Cottage

Drayton Cottage, a semi-detached two-storey house which adjoins Sunnyside, is believed to date back around 150 years and to have been constructed of local brick. It is certain that cottages stood on this site as early as 1838 when they are listed on the Tithe Map and accompanying Apportionment Document, although it is possible that the original cottages were at some stage pulled down and replaced by the current buildings. Owned in 1838 by William Christopher/Jenney, the two cottages were rented at that time by the families of William Gurney and James Lovett, both agricultural labourers. William Gurney is named in the 1847 Drayton Church Book as being employed to weed the churchyard as well as working as an agricultural labourer. There had been Lovetts resident in Drayton Beauchamp and Gurneys resident in nearby villages as far back as 1798 when the Buckinghamshire Posse Comitatus was drawn up. The Lovetts continue to be listed in village records for a further seventy years after 1838 and the Gurneys for a further fifty years although, as explained in the Introduction to this book, it is unfortunately impossible to be certain about addresses.

The histories of Drayton Cottage and Sunnyside since the beginning of the twentieth century are closely linked as described more fully under the Sunnyside heading. Both were bought from the Jenney estate between 1917 and 1935 by Joseph Kempster who gave one (presumably Sunnyside) to his son Walter and the other (presumably Drayton Cottage) to his daughter Edith. Edith and her husband Tom lived in Drayton Cottage for at least ten years after marrying in 1924. In 1945 the cottage was still being called "Kempster's Cottages" in the Electoral Register, but whether this was because the Kempster family still owned the cottage or simply a continuing use of the traditional name is not known. It is first listed as Drayton Cottage on the 1953 Electoral Register.

Alan and Esmé Southam

In October 1964 Alan and Esmé Southam, newly married, moved to Drayton Cottage, buying the house from James and Amy Shipperley who had lived there for around ten years.

Alan originated from Rickmansworth and Esmé from Remenham Hill near Henley-on-Thames. Drayton Beauchamp attracted them as house prices were cheaper than for properties closer to London, and the village was within ideal commuting distance of Berkhamsted where Alan was working as transport manager for Coopers of Berkhamsted. Subsequently he worked for the Prudential for a time before setting up his own mechanical business. Esmé was trained in office work, meeting Alan when she and a girl friend went dancing at Wembley Town Hall. At that point she was living with her aunt and uncle in Kenton near Harrow-on-the-Hill and doing secretarial work for her uncle who was Export Director for H & T

Kirby and Co. Ltd., a firm of manufacturing chemists. After she and Alan moved to Drayton Beauchamp, Esmé worked for a time for East & Son Ltd, a timber company in Berkhamsted, as she was now living too far away to continue to commute to her previous place of work.

Drayton Cottage was first modernised around 1956 when an indoor bathroom was constructed on the ground floor and a septic tank installed to replace the outside privy which had previously discharged into a drainage ditch in the field behind the cottages. Alan and Esmé added a porch and brick garage soon after they moved in, the work being done by Alan and his father. A bedroom was created in the loft, and around 1970 Alan and Wally Kempster had the roofs of both Drayton Cottage and Sunnyside retiled. The kitchen was extended and a wood-burning stove replaced the original fireplace which still had the rungs used by the chimneysweep boys as they climbed the chimney.

The couple's two daughters were born at the Royal Buckinghamshire Hospital in Aylesbury in 1969 and 1972 and spent their childhood in Drayton Beauchamp. Alan and Esmé remained at Drayton Cottage for 36 years until in 2000 they moved to County Durham where one daughter by then lived and where they had enjoyed caravan holidays for many years.

Sadly, Alan died suddenly only three years later. Esmé remains in the house in County Durham to which they retired, not far from her daughter, son-in-law and three small grandchildren. (Her other daughter is married and living in Quainton.) Esmé remembers Drayton Beauchamp as a village where people were in general friendly, but as a smaller place than it was by the time she moved away, with so many barns having by then been converted into homes. She recalls sociable Harvest Festivals when villagers enjoyed the hospitality of Dr Adams who erected a marquee in the garden of The Old Rectory. Alan was very happy working in his own business with many local contacts, and was known to everyone in the village as a skilled repairer of all things mechanical.

Don and Tracey Bailey

After Alan and Esmé moved away in 2000, another family lived at Drayton Cottage until November 2004 when the property was sold to Don and Tracey Bailey, the current owners.

At that time, the cottage had only two bedrooms and a log-burning stove with a back boiler to provide heating and hot water. In early 2006 the couple, by now with a small child, moved out for almost a year while a major programme of modernisation and extension was carried out. The cottage, which sits on a quarter-of-an-acre plot backing on to fields, now has five bedrooms, three public rooms, and modern amenities.

Don Bailey originates from Hatfield and Tracey from Pinner. In 2001 Don changed careers from consultant surveyor to property developer, moving from London to Hemel Hempstead. He and Tracey met through work as Tracey was employed in administration in the property business. The two lived in Hertford, but knew and liked the area around Drayton Beauchamp. They recognised the potential of Drayton Cottage which already had planning approval for an extension. Both of their families live within a reasonable distance of Drayton Beauchamp and the village is within comfortable commuting distance for Don by train from Wendover. The couple now have a young son and daughter and hope that both children will be able to complete their education up to secondary school age at Wendover First and Middle Schools.

The family are happy in the village whose quiet rural setting is, they feel, ideal for raising children. They recognise, however, that extra effort is required to get to know other villagers because of the lack of a central meeting-point and the fact that most people enter and leave the village by car. Walking their dog has proved to be a good way of meeting other residents, however, and village events such as the Parish Meeting and the recent "walking of the parish boundaries" are excellent ways to encourage villagers to come together and discover common interests. The Baileys would hope not to move from the village unless the children are unable to secure places in due course at the highly-rated Wendover Middle School, outside whose catchment area Drayton Beauchamp unfortunately lies.

DRAYTON COTTAGE

SUNNYSIDE   Ethel Kempster

David Ballad, Margaret Dean & Richard Gregory

Sunnyside

As outlined in the previous chapter, Drayton Cottage and Sunnyside are likely to have been constructed at the same time. For many years attached to Morgans Farm, they were used to house farm workers employed there.

Walter and Ethel Kempster

The history of Sunnyside is inextricably bound up with that of the Kempster family, part of the large extended Kempster family of Buckinghamshire and Hertfordshire. One branch of this family seems to have moved to Drayton Beauchamp between 1892 and 1897. Even earlier, however, the village church's Marriage Register records the marriage in Drayton Beauchamp in 1726 of Sarah Kempster to John Waters and in 1762 the marriage of Joseph Kempster of Marsworth to Mary Coker of Drayton Beauchamp.

In the 1901 Census, Joseph Kempster (43), a labourer, was living in the so-called "Village Road", Drayton Beauchamp along with his wife Esther (44) and their children Walter (18), who was a labourer, Robert (14), a domestic houseboy, Edith (9) and Ernest Thomas (4). All had been born in Wilstone apart from Ernest who was born in Drayton Beauchamp. Esther's family, the Oakleys, seem to have lived in and around Whittle Farm and Draytonmead Farm which, although more or less in Puttenham, were also traditionally outlying parts of Drayton Beauchamp parish. Both farms belonged to the Jenney estate and both were sold by Stewart William Jenney in 1917.

In the 1911 Census the Kempster family are again listed as living in Drayton Beauchamp, but with no address given. By this time, the fourteen-year-old Ernest is described as being employed as a "boy on farm". He was killed, a lad of only nineteen, when HMS Queen Mary was blown up during the Battle of Jutland in 1916 and he is commemorated both on the Peace Memorial in the village church and on the Navy Memorial on Southsea Common.

The oldest child of Joseph and Esther was Alice. After working for some time in Hemel Hempstead, Alice in 1902 married David Rance, a widowed Army pensioner who had become a lock-keeper. By 1911 she was living with him and their five children at Lock Cottage, Drayton Beauchamp.

Joseph lived until 1938, his wife Esther having died in 1903. He seems from the Jenney archives to have lived for some time in one of the "Mansion Cottages" - i.e. the Dower House - and was definitely there in 1903, but he was no longer a tenant there by 1912 and at some point between 1917 and 1935 he bought the two cottages – now called Sunnyside and Drayton Cottage – from the Jenney estate for £100 each. It may be that he purchased them from Stewart William Jenney in 1919 when the latter sold Morgans Farm to Leonard Lewin. The fact that the cottages are not mentioned as part of the sale of Morgans Farm in 1919 or when it was advertised again for auction in 1925 would give strength to this hypothesis. (A poignant letter written by Joseph to Stewart William Jenney in May 1916 asks that the troublesome chimney on his cottage should be repaired. The repair had still not been carried out by Christmas of that year although it was planned that a cowl should be provided and fixed on the chimney.) After buying the two cottages, Joseph gave one to his son Walter and the other to his daughter Edith and they became known as Kempsters Cottages. Edith married Thomas Reeves in 1924. She died in 1952 and he ten years later.

Joseph's son Walter, born in 1883, emigrated to Canada on the Allen Line ship HMS Virginian in 1914. He may well have been intending to farm in Saskatchewan or Alberta under a scheme whereby, to encourage settlement in the Prairies, the Dominion Government was offering plots of 160 acres free for a $10 registration fee to British subjects or naturalised British subjects over 21 years of age. To receive the patent for the land, they had to be willing to cultivate at least thirty of the 160 acres over three years of hard work and to build a house on the plot worth at least $300.

On 7th January 1915 Walter enlisted with the Canadian Overseas Expeditionary Force in Edmonton, Alberta. Intriguingly an Arthur Kempster of Wingrave (ten years younger than Walter and a butcher by trade) enlisted at Beeching Stoke, Wiltshire, with the 3rd Canadian Field Artillery on exactly the same day as Walter. This seems beyond coincidence, but so far it has not been possible to trace with certainty the relationship between the two men. Sadly, Arthur Kempster died on 19th November 1918 just after the Armistice and aged only 25. His grave is in a Wingrave churchyard and his name is on the Canadian Roll of Honour.

After the Armistice Walter returned to Canada on the White Star Line ship RMS Olympic (sister ship to the Titanic) which was serving as a troopship, but within five years he came back to Drayton Beauchamp and in 1921 married Ellen, a London girl. He died in 1929, when his son Walter (known locally as "Wally") was only six years old.

As a boy Wally Kempster sang in the village choir, and later recounted to his wife stories of how, to keep himself awake during the long sermons, he would dig his thumbs into the pew in front of him, or amuse himself with the other boys by throwing missiles at each other across the aisle when the Rector was facing the congregation. It has been possible to establish that Wally, as well as being a good friend of the twin brothers of Betty Kempster whose family lived at the thatched Cottage, was also closely related on both sides of his family to Betty's branch of the Kempster family.

Wally served in the Royal Army Service Corps during World War II, returning in 1945. In 1954 he married Ethel, born in Berkhamsted. Ethel changed the name of the cottage to Sunnyside to end the confusion of having so many occurrences of the name "Kempster" in the village. Ellen Kempster continued to live with her son and daughter-in-law until she died in 1965. Wally, a much-loved figure in the village, died in 1998 in the room in which he was born. Ethel continues to live in Sunnyside. The couple's twin sons Alan and Arthur, born in 1960, live within five miles of her and are frequent visitors.

Sunnyside originally had one sitting room and a kitchen downstairs and two bedrooms upstairs. As a young bride, Ethel hated the earth privy at the end of the garden. Wally dug a cesspit to create an indoor toilet, and added a kitchen and sitting room so that he and Ethel had some private space separate from his mother's accommodation. The cottage backs on to fields and looks towards the reservoir. It is believed that there used to be a bakery in front of the cottage and close to the village lane, but this had disappeared by 1954 when Ethel arrived.

Ethel and Wally both worked at Apsley Paper Mills and commuted by Lambretta, resorting to using the train for part of the journey when winter weather made the ride unbearable. Their sons, born (because they were twins) in Aylesbury rather than at home, were brought up as country lads and have many memories of the Drayton Beauchamp of their childhood. Alan, for instance, can remember that they would help to feed the pigs which were kept in what is now Long Barn. Wearing wellington boots, they would stand on the rail and compete to see which of them could bear for longer the pain of the pigs nipping their toes.

There are amusing memories too of the Ballad sisters who were still clinging to their Morris Oxford car, registration number SBH 3, despite the dangerously deteriorating eyesight of the only sister who could drive. Ultimately, Wally drove the car for them but was reminded constantly by his elderly passengers that any speed over 40 mph was "too fast". After retirement, Wally was a loyal helper of the by-then elderly Bill Oliphant of Morgans. He also wrote poetry, encouraged by fellow poet Norma Anns of 2 Peartree Cottages.

Ethel's first memory of the village was of coming with Wally on the bus from Berkhamsted to the top of the Holloway and then walking with him down through the village to meet his mother. Initially she thought he was playing a joke on her and she simply could not imagine ever living in such an isolated place. When she moved to the village, Ethel not surprisingly found it very quiet after life in busy Berkhamsted, but she settled in time, and knew in any case that Wally would never want to leave Drayton Beauchamp. She is content now with her peaceful life and has no plans to move or to make further changes to the house in which she has lived for 57 years.

Genista

Now a substantial brick-built single dwelling, Genista is believed to date from the early 1700s. In the 1910 register of "Duties on Land Values", the owner of what were then two cottages was given as Harry Dwight of Upper Farm. By 1925 they seem to have been sold to the owner of Morgans Farm and in that year were put up for auction by Leslie Webb. It is possible that they were bought back by Harry Dwight of Upper Farm for the use of his farm workers as the two cottages subsequently became known as Upper Farm Cottages. The original cottages were "two up-two down" residences with outside privies although an extension was added to the rear of both cottages during the Victorian era.

In the 1838 Parish Tithe Map and Apportionment Document, the cottages and Upper Farm itself were owned, not surprisingly, by William Christopher/Jenney. The tenants of the two cottages were Thomas Parkin and Joseph Ricketts. In the 1841 Census, Thomas Parkin was 45, an agricultural labourer married to Mary (43) and sharing the cottage - at least on the night of the census - with Charlotte Timpson (16) and Martha Clark (2). The Parkin family is not mentioned in later censuses.

In the 1841 Census, Joseph Ricketts was 45, a farm labourer, married to Martha [elsewhere called Maria] (40) and with children Ann (20), William (18), and Sophia (12). The Ricketts family appear to have moved to Drayton Beauchamp from Wilstone sometime between 1818 and 1826 and had at least five children. One, Ann, married Robert Howlett of Moat Cottage in 1849. Another, Joseph, married Mary Ann Lovett in 1850, Mary Ann being a daughter of James Lovett of Drayton Cottage. These two marriages, then, connected three of the principal village families – the Howletts, Ricketts and Lovetts. The Kelly's Post Office Directory of 1854 lists Joseph Ricketts as organist at the village church, but whether this is father or son is not stated.

Joseph and Mary Ann Ricketts must have moved to Rectory Cottage at some point after their marriage as the church Burial Register lists their son William as dying in 1856 at seven weeks of age and Mary Ann herself dying only three weeks later aged 26. Albert Ricketts aged seventeen (William's cousin) died in 1871, and is recorded as having "drowned bathing". Albert, Joseph's grandson, was a son of Caleb and Rebecca Ricketts who were at that time living at Mansion Meadows (i.e. The Dower House). Whether he was swimming in the canal, in one of the village ponds, or in the recently-created Wilstone Reservoir is not documented. The Ricketts family continues to be mentioned in church records into the twentieth century.

In 1946, Upper Farm and its two cottages were sold by John and Mabel Biggs to Harry and Rebecca Nicholls of Tring Grange Farm, the grandparents of the

1 PEARTREE COTTAGES

Ron & Tracey West

2 PEARTREE COTTAGES

Norma & Michael Anns

UPPER FARM

Margaret & Gordon Nicholls

present-day farmer, Gordon Nicholls. A succession of people are listed on the Electoral Registers as living at Upper Farm Cottages between 1946 and 1977 – among them in 1963 Mick and Janet Anns (Mick having been born nearby at 2 Peartree Cottages). By coincidence, Mick's aunt – Amy Sylvia Ball – also lived for several years in the Upper Farm Cottage which stands the further away of the two from the farm. Having married Stanley Gregory, Sylvia lived with her sister Margery in 2 Peartree Cottages during the war and until 1947 while their two husbands were serving in the Armed Forces. After a spell in Rose Cottages across the village lane, she, her husband and their two children (Richard and Margaret, whose account of village life appears elsewhere in this book) moved to Upper Farm Cottages until 1955/6 when the family moved to New Mill. Sylvia and Stanley are both buried in the village churchyard.

By 1954 the cottage nearer Upper Farm was being rented by Michael Hannon, a builder. After the Gregory family moved away he was authorised to turn the two cottages into one house which was lived in for ten years by Sheila and Harold Nicholls before being sold in 1977 by the Nicholls family to John and Jean Welford of Kingston-upon-Thames who renamed it "Genista".

A final extension was added to Genista in 2001, converting the garage into a suite of rooms. There are now "six plus" bedrooms and four public rooms.

Martin and Fiona Green

In 1991 the Welfords moved to France, selling Genista to Martin and Catherine Green who moved in with their two-year-old daughter, Harriet, in 1992. The Greens' son Tom was born later that year. The Greens' marriage ended in 1995 and Martin has subsequently married Fiona, raised in Cheltenham but working in London. Martin, a merchant banker, was born and brought up in London.

Martin and Fiona like the village immensely and consider it in the main a very attractive place. They enjoy beautiful views from the rear windows of their house and would hate to see any significant development which would threaten to ruin the tranquillity and character of what is still a relatively unspoilt village. They strongly dislike the A41 bypass with the "butchery of the countryside" which its construction has caused, even although the new road may have shortened the travel time to London. They find the village a friendly but not claustrophobic place, and feel it would be given a fresh lease of life if some younger families were to move in.

Peartree Cottages

The exact age of the two Peartree Cottages is not known. Interestingly, however, a coin dating back to the 1800s was found when a new floor was laid at number 2, and there is an earth floor under the red and black tiles of the sitting room there. Bricks used in the construction of the cottages are believed to be at least 200 years old, and cottages are shown on the same site on the 1736 "Mapp of the Mannour of Drayton Beauchamp".

The two cottages originally belonged to Upper Farm but at some point between 1927 and 1944 must have been bought by George MacDonald Brown of Morgan's Farm. In 1955 Aylesbury Rural District Council purchased the two Peartree Cottages from the executors of his estate. The original staircases which had led up from the kitchen were blocked up and re-sited (although a ghostly couple have been seen on occasion "climbing up" the original stairs at number 2), and a small extension was added to each cottage by the building firm James Chandler & Co. of Long Marston. The front door at number 2 was also re-positioned and the original door became a window. Both 1 and 2 Peartree Cottages are now owned by The Vale of Aylesbury Housing Trust which took over from the Council approximately nine years ago. The most recent changes at number 2 have been the building of a conservatory in 1999 and the conversion of the downstairs bathroom into a "wet room".

1 Peartree Cottages

Ron and Tracey West

Ron and Tracey West, who have lived at 1 Peartree Cottages since January 1986, have made some improvements to their cottage – a new kitchen, shower room and conservatory, for instance – but it retains its original "two up-two down" configuration.

Ron and Tracey and their four-year-old-son moved into the cottage a few months after the previous tenant, Eugene (Betty) Jones, had moved to Oxford. Their daughter was born three years later and still lives at home, driving herself to work in Hemel Hempstead. She, having been born in Aylesbury and having lived in the village all her life, is fiercely attached to Drayton Beauchamp and would not like to move away. As did (and still do) many of the village children, she and her brother were taken to and from school by taxi or school bus, depending on the destination. As there are no pavements throughout Drayton Beauchamp, between the village and the Tring Hill roundabout, or on the Lower Icknield Way as far as the Buckland crossroads, it would nowadays be deemed unsafe to have children walking from the village to school – although in earlier times even the youngest village children walked every day unaccompanied to school in Wilstone or Aston Clinton.

Ron originates from Solihull and Tracey from Coventry, and the couple were living in the centre of Coventry before moving to the rural isolation of Drayton Beauchamp. Ron worked as a coach driver and his employer wanted him to work from the company's Aylesbury base. They knew no-one locally when they moved here and had no alternative but to ask the Council for help with housing.

Tracey, as a newcomer to the village, initially felt lonely and homesick, particularly as she does not drive and Ron was away for long stretches driving coaches abroad and with only a few days at home in between trips. In Coventry she could walk or take public transport to shops and other facilities. Since moving here she has continued to walk – a necessity when public transport is unreliable, expensive and infrequent. When they arrived they were befriended by Margery Anns next door at 2 Peartree Cottages and they remember her with great affection. Their neighbours on the other side at Genista were Paul and Jean Welford who then moved to France. Ron and Tracey now have a good circle of local friends and feel well settled, with no plans to move elsewhere.

Ron retired in 2005 because of ill health, and he and Tracey enjoy reading, walking, dog-sitting and gardening. At the same time, they feel that the quality of life in the village would be improved if there were both a more reliable and affordable public transport system and a local meeting place – like a hall - where

Noreen & Anne Hannon, Mandy Beckett &
Margaret Gregory c.1959

Thatched Cottage beside Terriers End

THE MOAT HOUSE during construction 1951

Charles Bradshaw, Fred Bryant, Alfred Hearn
& Peter Smith at Painesend Farm c.1951

Ploughing in Drayton Beauchamp c.1920

Sarah & Frank Harrowell at Yew Tree c.1920

Betty Kempster at birthplace in The Cottage

Doris & Wally Kempster c.1947

villagers could get together to socialise. They regret the apparent loss of a traditional village way of life when neighbours would look out for each other and when doors would be left open to welcome all visitors. In the winter particularly, villagers now withdraw into their houses and days can pass without a single person being seen walking along the lane. A further improvement would be to dig out thoroughly the stream which runs through the village rather than to leave it as the rather overgrown and sluggish stretch of water, prone to overflowing, which we currently have. A final valuable development would be if some solution could be found for the perennial problem of traffic cutting through the village at high speed.

2 Peartree Cottages

(Michael) Mick and Norma Anns

"Ball" is one of the most frequently-encountered surnames in village archives, and members of the Ball family have, at one time or another, lived in virtually every house in the main part of the village.

The Ball name appears in Drayton Beauchamp as early as 1817 when Henry Ball and his wife Sarah had their son William Henry baptised in the village church although the family were living in Buckland. There must have been strong connections between the branches of the family living in the villages of Buckland, Puttenham, Wilstone and Drayton Beauchamp as church records list a succession of baptisms, marriages and burials of Balls living in these villages.

In 1838 the Tithe Map lists Henry Ball as being a tenant of William Christopher at one of the Peartree Cottages. In the 1841 Census, Henry is still there, now 45 and with a wife Ann, 35, and children Abel, seventeen, Elizabeth twelve, and the one-year-old Mary Ann.

George Ball (born in Puttenham) and his wife Ann (née Hedges), who had been born in Buckland, married in 1847 in Drayton Beauchamp church and had four children together. Their third child, Walter, born in 1857, married Elizabeth (née Green) in 1877. Elizabeth and Walter had seven children, five of whom appear along with other descendants of the couple in a photograph published in the Bucks Herald in November 1959 on the occasion of Elizabeth's 102nd birthday.

The fourth son of Elizabeth and Walter was Arthur George, whose daughter is Ruth Akerman – also an invaluable contributor to this book.

The third child born to Elizabeth and Walter was Edgar who married Amy Amelia (née Proctor) of Puttenham. Edgar and Amy had a son Edgar, born in 1906. Little Edgar, always known as Billy, seemed perfectly healthy as a baby, but eventually proved to be severely disabled, and was totally dependent on his mother until he died in 1952. His disabilities have always been linked in the minds of his family with the vaccinations he had had as a baby. Edgar and Amy also had two daughters - Amy Sylvia, born in 1912, and Margery, born in 1916. Amy Sylvia was the mother of Richard Gregory and Margaret Dean, whose contribution to this project also appears elsewhere. Margery was Mick Anns' mother.

Mick's father, Jim Anns, moved to Drayton Beauchamp around 1937 from East Hendred in Berkshire to work for Captain MacDonald Brown as the butler at

Morgans Farm. There he met Margery Ball, employed as a maid at the farm. The two married in 1939 and moved into 2 Peartree Cottages. The following year Mick, their only child, was born in one of the two upstairs bedrooms there. Jim Anns went off to the War exactly a week later and did not return for five years. 2 Peartree Cottages was commandeered during the war by the RAF who housed officers there.   After his return Jim worked at Moorhouse's Jam Factory in Aylesbury and then at Moat House where he was gardener and finally at Broadview Farm where he helped with the pigs. He also looked after the village churchyard for fifteen years from 1965-80.

In his father's absence, Mick was brought up by his mother, aunts and grandmother.   Other Ball relatives lived all around and Mick knew – and was known by – everyone in the village. From an early age (and often when he should really have been at school) he helped at Upper Farm, first when John Biggs was farmer there and then when Harry Nicholls took over. He pumped the village church organ on Sundays and went on Saturday afternoon "jaunts" with his friends John Spittles and Pete Knight who occasionally used to "borrow" the pony and trap belonging to the Ballads at Lower Farm. A favourite destination was the rookery at Buckland where, at bird-nesting time, rooks' eggs could be collected. Mick remembers village parties at the Dower House when Alfred Reynolds and his sister lived there, and he appears on both of the village group photographs taken in the late 1940s.   Mick, his cousin Richard Gregory and his friend John Spittles from Rectory Farm sometimes used a push-mower to mow a cricket pitch in one of the Ballads' level fields and the boys would crawl through a fence to take eggs from a hen house to cook in a hole dug in a field. The workers on the various farms – and the village women busy around their cottages – would keep an eye on children like Mick, making sure they came to no harm but allowing them freedom to explore the countryside. The schoolhouse was at that time used as a village hall and Mick recalls watching the 1953 Coronation there on a television hired by villagers for the occasion. Indeed Mick's mother was born at the schoolhouse, her parents having moved there from the Dower House before later moving to the thatched Cottage at the far end of the village, next door to Betty Kempster and her family.

When Mick's mother Margery was a child, a tiny shop still existed in the front room of one of the cottages which is now part of Badgers End. The pump and well outside would have provided a regular meeting-place for villagers.   Mick's grandmother plaited straw for the hat industry in Luton, as did a decreasing number of the village women at that time. There had been no water in the canal within living memory, and crockery and other rubbish would be thrown under the bridge by villagers as they passed. There were no high hedges in front of any of the cottages. This perhaps resulted in some loss of privacy, but was more than compensated for by the ready socialising between villagers and the immediate help that could be counted on in times of trouble.

Mick's first paid work was for Harry Nicholls at Upper Farm. He then took up bricklaying and building, studying at Aylesbury Technical College, and working on the construction of the new town of Hemel Hempstead. He was a carpenter at Grossmith in Aston Clinton, making chicken cages, and then worked in Tring as a slaughterman for Frovines. In 1974 he took over a huge greenhouse which had been erected in what is now the back garden of Long Barn. Backed by Bill Oliphant, Mick grew tomatoes and hoped to establish a market garden. Sadly, his first marriage was ending so he stopped using the greenhouse – ironically just before the start of his relationship with Norma, now his second wife, who comes from a family of enthusiastic smallholders and market gardeners.

Mick and Norma (who comes from Bucknell, Oxfordshire) first met in 1972 but Norma's father and Mick had worked together several years earlier. For a time they lived in Wing and in Bracknell near Bicester. In 1996 they returned to 2 Peartree Cottages to look after Mick's mother Margery who could no longer manage alone. (Margery died in 2000; her husband Jim had died in 1983.) Mick has two adult daughters and Norma has one daughter. All live independently away from Drayton Beauchamp but are in close and frequent contact with Mick and Norma.

Norma and Mick have no thought of leaving the village and intend to be buried along with Mick's ancestors. Even so, they feel with some regret that the village has changed enormously over the past sixty years from the farming village is used to be. Most residents are not country people but have moved here from the towns because they can afford to buy the large properties which have been converted from old cottages and barns. The old easy socialising among the farm workers' families has gone and some residents are rarely seen.

Richard Gregory and Margaret Dean (Née Gregory)

Richard and Margaret are the children of Amy Sylvia and Stanley Gregory. Their mother - always called Sylvia - was the older daughter of Amy and Edgar Ball and the godmother of Betty Kempster whose family lived next door to the Balls in the 1930s in the other half of the thatched Cottage. A wedding photograph of 1937 of Sylvia and Stanley clearly shows the Cottage in the background.

The children's father, then in his thirties, was working as a baker in Long Marston – and thus in a reserved occupation - when World War II began, but he joined the RAF and saw active service in Europe. Sylvia returned to Drayton Beauchamp to be close to her family while he was abroad.

Richard was born in 1944 at 2 Peartree Cottages, the home of his Aunt Margery and her son Mick (Anns). Margery's husband Jim was also serving in the Forces abroad at the time so it is likely that the two sisters lived together for companionship while the men were away. By 1947 when Richard's sister Margaret was born, the family were living across the village lane in one of the Rose Cottages which belonged to Lower Farm and which were eventually converted into the house now known as Badgers End. At some point the Gregorys moved over the lane to Upper Farm Cottages, next door to the Kempster family.

Margaret and Richard have vivid memories of the village and its residents (to several of whom they were related) from their childhood years. In the other half of Rose Cottages were Caroline Rainbow, her daughter Mary Stillwell and Mary's son Roger. (Mary's husband Harry was serving in the Royal Navy.) Bill and Iris Cato lived in Upper Farm Cottages and were followed by Maureen and Michael Hannon who had previously lived in one of the thatched cottages owned by Morgans Farm at the lower end of the village. Michael, a builder, knocked down walls in Upper Farm Cottages to convert the two into one house. In 1967 Sheila and Harold Nicholls moved there, staying for ten years and having two children – a son and a daughter – during this time. In 1977 the house was sold by the Nicholls family to Jean and Paul Welford and renamed "Genista". Across the fence in Kempster's Cottages (Sunnyside) were Ellen Kempster and her son Wally, and later Wally's wife Ethel. Harry Nicholls (who called Margaret Gregory "Topsy" and who was Gordon Nicholls's grandfather) was at Upper Farm and the Gregory children used to admire the heavy crops of apples in the paddock and the grapes against the farmhouse wall. Their Aunt Margery worked for Harry for many years. Richard can remember his uncle, Jim Anns, working at the Moat House and helping to lay out rose beds there.

When Richard and Margaret were children, their maternal grandparents Amy and Edgar Ball were living at Beauchamp Cottages (at the side nearer Drayton Cottage), with Charlotte and Walter Hedges in the adjoining cottage. Margaret can remember going with her Aunt Margery in the mid-1950s to pay the rent for 2 Peartree Cottages at the Brown and Merry offices in Tring. This would have been just before the two Peartree Cottages and both Beauchamp Cottages were sold to Aylesbury Rural District Council in July 1955. Whilst the demolition and rebuilding of Beauchamp Cottages was going on, the Hedges lived across the village lane at one of the Ballad Cottages (now half of Setherwood), moving back to the newly rebuilt number 1 Beauchamp Cottages in 1957. Amy and Edgar Ball and their son Billy must have moved elsewhere during the rebuilding too but it is not certain where this was. When the new bungalows were finished Amy, Edgar and Billy returned to the new number 2 Beauchamp Cottages, next door neighbours once again to the Hedges.

At this time, the Ballad sisters Florence and Edith and their brother Fred were still living and working at Lower Farm until Fred died in 1957. Their nephew Gordon lived at Rye Hill Farm and came down daily by tractor to visit his aunts until they sold Lower Farm in 1959. At Drayton Cottage were Nellie and John Wheatley. Gladys Chapman lived at Church Hill Farm (always called "Chapman's Farm") which Margaret and Richard remember as a small working farm with a large Dutch barn. Maria and William Hurst lived at The Cottage (listed in the Electoral Register of 1954 as 1 Morgans Farm Cottages.) Maria worked for Bill Oliphant at Morgans Farm and William worked at the cement works at Pitstone. In number 2 lived Betty Zywczynski.

Richard and Margaret attended primary school in Aston Clinton, being taken to and fro by taxi. In those days the girls' school building – since demolished - was beside the Anthony Hall, while the boys were taught on the opposite side of the road in the old building with the clock tower.

There were several boys of around Richard's age in the village in the 1950s but no other girls of Margaret's age, so she was often obliged to "tag along" with the boys – something which neither they nor she enjoyed. She did, however, enjoy playing with the two little Hannon girls, Ann and Noreen, and with Mandy Beckett, although all were younger than she. Village children spent many hours fishing in the moats which were netted and stocked with fish, and Richard recalls having two accidents there. In the first, he fell into the water and was rescued by Harry Nicholls who fished him out with a long implement meant for weeding. In the other, he became stuck in the muddy water at the edge of the moat and escaped only by leaving his wellington boots behind. He imagines that the boots must still lie somewhere in the mud. Both Richard and Margaret have vivid memories of a bicycle frame with no tyres which Richard, their cousin Mick Anns, and their friend Bob Menday from Ryecote found in the Tring rubbish dump which was at that time still near the village on the side of the canal. The "bicycle" was borne home to Margaret who with great determination learned to ride it. Margaret still remembers too the delight of sitting beside the milk roundsman, Jim Fowler, as he delivered milk in the village with his horse and cart and the excitement of the mobile shops – particularly Gower's van which seemed to stock everything imaginable.

Richard and Margaret remember attending a Coronation party in 1953 either at the schoolhouse or outside the church, and a party at the Dower House hosted by Alfred Reynolds. Margaret also recalls being taught how to curtsey in preparation for presenting a bouquet to "someone" (identity now forgotten) in the gardens of the Rectory when she was around seven years old. This dignitary may have been the wife of the Bishop of Oxford who on at least one occasion came with her husband to the Harvest Thanksgiving service in the village church followed by a tea party at the Rectory.

During their childhood there was still an afternoon service on Sundays in the village church, and there was still a shop at Bucklandwharf.

After the war, their father became a butcher and the family moved in 1955/6 to New Mill, Tring. Richard followed his father into the family business. Neither Richard nor Margaret has subsequently returned to live in Drayton Beauchamp. Margaret in particular, however, has maintained her links with Drayton Beauchamp, and continues to attend services at the village church. Their parents, Sylvia and Stanley, are both buried in the village churchyard.

Looking back to their parents' and grandparents' times, Richard and Margaret are struck by how hard the villagers of previous generations had to work, even as children – long hours, much physical labour, and few "aids" to make their lives easier. People then did not "go away" on holiday, but thought it a great treat to spend a day at the reservoir where the water and the sandy area at the edge provided a fine alternative to a seaside outing.

Garth Beckett digging drive at 1 Peartree Cottages c.1959

Margery, Amy & Billy Ball c.1918

Stanley Gregory, Sylvia Ball & bridesmaid Margery Ball 1937

Frank John Hedges (Jack) c.1895 aged 3 years

Painesend Farm 2009 before demolition

Peter Smith & grandmother Ellen & uncle Fred c.1942

Jean & John Brown at Applewood

David & Sue Whinyates & Family

Betty Beckett at 'Devereux'

Upper Farm

Upper Farm dates back to the seventeenth century and is a Grade II listed brick building. The farmhouse now has a traditional clay tile roof, but the remains of the original thatched roof can still be seen among the substantial oak beams and gables on top of which a new roof was constructed in 1913. As with Lower Farm and Morgans/Old Manor Farm, the farmhouse of Upper Farm sits sideways on to the village lane. The most practical explanation for this is that by positioning the farmhouse in this way, the space was fully utilised, the living room overlooked the central courtyard, and the farmer could keep a watchful eye on the work being done without needing to be out-of-doors constantly himself.

Upper Farm is clearly depicted on a hand-painted "Mapp of the Mannour of Drayton Beauchamp" dated 1736. It also appears on the 1838 Tithe Map and accompanying document at which time the farm and 154 acres were owned by William Christopher/Jenney of Drayton Lodge and tenanted by Thomas Griffin. One of the menservants at Upper Farm in the 1841 Census was John Cyster, the fifteen-year-old son of Samuel and Sarah Cyster of Terriers End. Of interest too is the fact that listed at Upper Farm on the 1871 Census as an under-shepherd was Joseph, the thirteen-year-old son of Ann and Robert Stratford of the tiny schoolhouse. Joseph was the eighth of their twelve children so it must have been a considerable relief that the payment for his work included the provision of accommodation.

William Christopher also owned the two cottages which became known as "Upper Farm Cottages", and whose tenants in 1838 were Thomas Parkin and Joseph Ricketts. This was still the case by the time of the 1841 Census, but in the 1851 Census very few addresses are given so it is impossible to be certain who was living in the farm cottages. Richard Horwood is, however, named as the farmer at Upper Farm, employing ten men and five boys to help him with the farm which had grown to 240 acres. Richard Horwood remained at Upper Farm until his death aged 71 in 1881, his son by this stage being named as the co-tenant. By 1898 Richard Horwood the younger, a frequent winner of prizes for his animals, crops and farm produce, was in charge of both Upper Farm and Rectory/Church Farm – the latter a smallholding on the glebe lands near the church and Rectory. A document of 1898 lists among the buildings at Upper Farm a "chaise house with granary over". In 1913, extensive alterations and additions were made by the Jenney estate to Upper Farm – a staircase was removed, a bathroom installed, a stable built, and the farmhouse roof covered "with tiles laid on hay".

On 25th March 1913 Thomas Frederick Dwight (of the family who owned the well-known Dwight Pheasantries until the First World War put an end to game shooting) is named as the new tenant of Upper Farm. In the same year it is noted in the Parish Meeting minutes that his younger brother Harry had been appointed as one of the village Overseers. In September 1915 Harry married Mary Speed, also from a farming background. Richard Horwood the younger, by then living in Aston Clinton, seems to have continued to farm the Upper Farm lands which by then comprised 214 acres until 1919 whilst Harry served with the Royal Engineers during the Great War. Harry's regiment left England in March 1916 for active service, and the concern of villagers was minuted at a Parish Meeting in March 1917 when it was announced that there had been no reply to a letter written on behalf of the Meeting to wish him well. After his eventual return from war service in 1919 Harry Dwight bought Upper Farm and 194 acres, the two Upper Farm Cottages and the two Peartree Cottages from the Tring solicitor Arthur Vaisey and the village Rector, the Reverend Henry Burkitt, who had been appointed to administer between them Stewart William Jenney's business affairs. By this stage George McDonald Brown, a Land Agent from Tring and the future owner of Morgans Farm, was also heavily involved in the running of the Jenney estate. Harry Dwight died in 1925 aged forty and is buried in the village churchyard.

At some point, the four farm cottages were sold to Morgans Farm and in 1926 were put up for auction by the executors for Leslie Webb. It may be that Brown & Merry retained ownership of the two Peartree Cottages and rented them out separately from Morgans Farm. In July 1955 they were sold by the National Provincial Bank, executors for George MacDonald Brown, to Aylesbury Rural District Council and became Local Authority properties (as they still are).

The other two cottages may have been bought back in 1926 by Harry Dwight's widow and his brother Thomas Frederick who died in 1930 aged 49. Certainly, they remained attached to Upper Farm until the present owner sold them in 1977 to Paul and Jean Welford. In the mid 1950s, the two cottages had been converted, as has already been described, into one house by Michael Hannon, a house builder who was also a tenant there. The converted single dwelling was renamed "Genista". (Interestingly, the Moat House was also owned by Upper Farm until it was sold by Harry Nicholls. This explains why the official right of way into the Moat House is actually in Church Meadow where a bridge leads from the field to the house.)

Harry and Mary Dwight carried out extensive renovations to the farmhouse in the 1920s, building on a kitchen and passageway. There are now four bedrooms in the farmhouse, a fifth bedroom having been converted into a bathroom. A range of farm buildings traditionally stood around the courtyard, with most of them still in place – a shed for young cattle, a milking shed, stables, a dairy, a cart hovel, and a thrashing barn which was in recent years restored by the Milton Keynes "Driveforce".

Upper Farm changed hands again in 1931 when it was bought by John and Mabel Biggs who remained there until 1948 when Harry Nicholls, grandfather of the present owner, bought it. Originally a hay trusser and carter who had been born in Aston Clinton, Harry fought in the Army in Germany during the First World War.

The requisitioning of his horses during this war meant that there was little work available in the post-war years in either trussing or carting. By the time Harry returned from Germany, his sons had moved to the Old Duke's Head at Buckland, a former pub which had a large orchard where some calves could be kept. Harry turned from trussing and carting to farming, taking over Cobblers Pits Farm on Aston Hill once the army moved out of their camp at the end of World War I. He moved from there to Vale Farm on Cholesbury Common and then to Tring Grange Farm between Cholesbury and Champneys. His son Cecil had by this time begun farming in his own right and returned to Vale Farm, subsequently also taking on Hawridge Court Farm.

During the Second World War Harry and Cecil were obliged, with the assistance of Land Girls, to plough their fields for the war effort as had been decreed by the War Act, despite the fact that the flinty, stony ground made the task an almost impossible and highly expensive exercise. The two men were the first in the area to have in the 1930s a Fordson tractor with iron wheels. By fitting up lights on it themselves, they were able to plough at night as well as in daylight. Cecil bought Park Farm, Aston Clinton, in February 1953 and moved there with his family.

Gordon and Margaret Nicholls

Gordon, the second of Cecil's four sons, was born at Vale Farm. In 1972, Gordon moved to Upper Farm, Drayton Beauchamp, on his marriage to Margaret, a Long Marston girl. The two had met through Margaret's brother who, like Gordon, was a keen motorcyclist. Margaret worked as a secretary to solicitors until 1975 and then for a Legal Costs Draftsman, finally retiring in 2006. One of her tasks as a farmer's wife was to help sort the cattle out on a Sunday evening for the Monday market in Tring, Bicester, Thame or Banbury (a very different era from nowadays when all of the Nicholls' cattle are transported to Wales to be sold as deadweight). Nowadays, Gordon and two of his brothers are in partnership, with farms at Buckland and Aston Clinton as well as Upper Farm in Drayton Beauchamp and a total of one thousand acres of mixed farming. Each farm is self-contained with a separate stock unit so there is no longer the need to cart animal food daily from one farm to another – a huge problem during bad winter weather.

Gordon cannot contemplate a time when he will retire from farming or move from Upper Farm. Farming has always been a major feature of his life and he recalls helping his father, Freddie Ballad and Harry Rainbow to combine the Ballads' fields around Lower Farm at an age when he should still have been attending school. He and Margaret like the quietness of the village although they see the lane now as a rat run with traffic going towards the Upper Icknield Way in the mornings and back in the evenings. They enjoy friendly relations with everyone in the village, and, as the Nicholls family have always done, participate in village celebrations. Harry Nicholls, for example, provided a barrel of beer for the village party to celebrate the Coronation in 1953, while Gordon and Margaret donated land on which to place a village seat to mark the Silver Jubilee of the Coronation in 1977 and a lamb to roast at the celebration party.

For their part, villagers are proud still to have a working farm in the centre of the community.

Postscript

"The village (of Drayton Beauchamp)......is pretty and rural, and consists of three farm houses and a dozen and a half of neat cottages in couples, each possessing a small garden. The place is watered by a clear rivulet."

(J J Sheahan – 1861 – History and Topography of Buckinghamshire)

"This is Drayton, remote from and yet so near to the incessant stream of life that passes along the old Roman way, the Akeman Street."

"A few children playing in the street, a housewife standing at her door, and a glimpse of a farmer's man on the top of a hay-rick, were all the evidences of life seen on passing through....The peacefulness was profound...."

(Harman, H – 1934 – Sketches of the Buckinghamshire Countryside: Memories of Drayton Beauchamp)

References

Books

Beckett, I F W (ed.) (1985) Buckinghamshire Record Society Volume 22 The Buckinghamshire Posse Comitatus Lists 1798.

Buckinghamshire Archaeological Society : Records of Buckinghamshire -Vols. 1 -50. Various papers.

Cassey Edward & Co (1865) History, Topography and Directory of Buckinghamshire, Cambridgeshire and Hertfordshire.

Chambers, R (1869) Book of Days.

Harman, H (1934) Sketches of the Buckinghamshire Countryside. Hunt Barnard & Co Aylesbury (Chapter XII – "Memories of Drayton Beauchamp").

Harrod, J G & Co. (1876) Royal County Directory of Buckinghamshire.

Kelly's Directories of Buckinghamshire (1847 – 1939).

Lewis, Samuel (ed.) (1848) A Topographical Dictionary of England.

Lipscomb, G (1847) The History and Antiquities of the County of Buckingham. Volume 3.

Mawer, A and Stenton F M (1925) The Place Names of Buckinghamshire. Cambridge University Press.

Mercer and Crocker (1871) Commercial Directory of Buckinghamshire.

Musson and Craven (1853) Commercial Directory of the County of Buckingham and the Town of Windsor.

Page, W. FSA (ed.) Reprinted 1969 from the original edition of 1925. A History of the County of Buckingham (Victoria County History) Volumes I-IV.

Pevsner, N and Williamson, E (1960) Penguin The Buildings of England.

Sheahan J J (1861) History and Topography of Buckinghamshire.

Whiteman, A (ed) (1986) Compton Census of 1676 . A Critical Edition. Oxford University Press .

Williams, Dr A and Martin, Prof G H (eds.) (2003) Great Domesday Book: A complete Translation Vol. 1 Alecto Historical Editions. The Folio Society London.

Documents, papers and correspondence located in the Centre for Buckinghamshire Studies, Aylesbury

Censuses for Drayton Beauchamp 1841-1911.

Copy of Court Rolls 5th May 1834 and 7th May 1838 .

Cottesloe Hundreds Land Tax Assessments 1830-32 .

Cottesloe Hundreds Militia Ballot List 1812.

Drayton Beauchamp Overseers' Accounts Books 1666-1837.

Drayton Beauchamp Parish Magazines December 1879-June 1887.

Drayton Church Book 1829-1918 (Churchwardens' Accounts).

Drayton Beauchamp Parish Meeting Minutes 1894-present day.

Drayton Beauchamp Rate Account Book 1936.

Duties on Land Values – Drayton Beauchamp 1910.

Records of Drayton Lodge Estate and Stewards' Papers 1855-1927.

Reports of the Commissioners appointed to enquire concerning charities and education. 1815-1835.

St Mary the Virgin Church, Drayton Beauchamp Registers of Baptisms from 1538, Marriages from 1541 and Burials from 1567.

Valuation Rolls for the Parish of Drayton Beauchamp 1907-1928.

Maps located in the Centre for Buckinghamshire Studies, Aylesbury

Mapp of the Mannour of Drayton Beauchamp 1736.

Plan of an estate in the parish of Drayton Beauchamp, property of Rt. Hon. Lady Robert Manners 1824.

Tithe Map for the Parish of Drayton Beauchamp and document setting out the Apportionment of the Rent Charges in lieu of Tithes 1838.

Ordnance Survey Maps 1877, 1899, 1980.

Websites

British History Online 1795 Isleworth:The Environs of Middlesex. Vol. 3 County of Middlesex.

British Newspapers 1800-1900 online (British Library).

Buckinghamshire County Council website – Unlocking Buckinghamshire's Past.

The Gentlemen's Magazine online.

The London Gazette online.

www.highways.gov.uk/roads/projects/10945.htm